the
MISSING LINK

the MISSING LINK

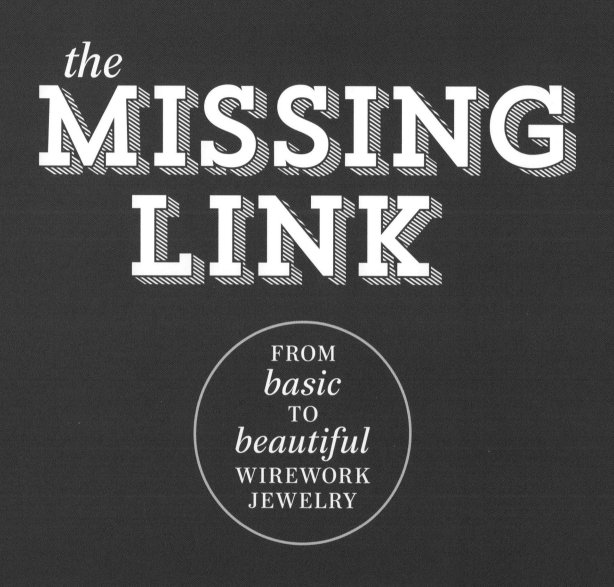

FROM *basic* TO *beautiful* WIREWORK JEWELRY

CINDY WIMMER

INTERWEAVE.
interweave.com

EDITOR Marlene Blessing

TECHNICAL EDITOR Jane Dickerson

ART DIRECTOR + DESIGNER Julia Boyles

PHOTOGRAPHER Joe Coca

HEAD SHOT Stephanie Dougher

PHOTO STYLIST Allie Liebgott

PRODUCTION DESIGNER Katherine Jackson

Interweave
A division of F+W Media, Inc.
201 East Fourth Street
Loveland, CO 80537
interweave.com

Manufactured in China
by RR Donnelley Shenzhen

Library of Congress
Cataloging-in-Publication Data

Wimmer, Cindy.

The missing link : from basic to beautiful
wirework jewelry / Cindy Wimmer.

pages cm

Includes index.

ISBN 978-1-59668-707-3 (pbk.)
ISBN 978-1-62033-024-1 (PDF)

1. Wire jewelry. 2. Wire craft. I. Title.

TT214.3.W566 2013

739.27'2--dc23

2013005857

10 9 8 7 6 5 4 3 2 1

DEDICATION

For the Wimmer Boys—Randy, Gabriel, Collin, Chandler, and Nathaniel. You fill my heart with pride and joy.

ACKNOWLEDGMENTS

As I reflect on this book-creating journey, I want to express special thanks and gratitude to my grandmother Rose, who taught me to value the work of our hands. I learned from her how to share what is in my heart by expressing it in handiwork.

Thank you to my family, who have been my biggest fans; your belief in me has inspired me to aim higher. Special thanks to my husband, Randy, who has stood by me in all of my creative endeavors and has always encouraged me wholeheartedly.

Thanks so much to my friends in the jewelry community. You have my appreciation for traveling this creative path alongside me, serving as mentors and friends. Your support gave me the green light I needed to pursue this book.

To Allison Korleski, my heartfelt thanks for believing in my book concept from the very beginning. You have been a source of guidance and support throughout the entire book-writing process.

Special thanks to my editor, Marlene Blessing. With your wisdom, I knew from day one that this project was in very capable hands. I experienced the best of work and play while in Colorado with you for the book photo shoot!

Thank you, Julia Boyles, for truly bringing my book to life with your design talent. To Joe Coca, thank you for your beautiful photography throughout the book. A special thank you to technical editor Jane Dickerson for your expertise.

To the entire team at Interweave—F+W Media, thank you for your talent and contributions in creating this book; I am incredibly grateful. And finally, my deepest appreciation to my contributing artists, Kerry Bogert, Christine Damm, Tracy Statler, Diane Cook, and Lori Anderson. Your designs add depth and beauty to *The Missing Link*.

CONTENTS

Now Starring: The Wire Links 32

Wire Links in Design 94

FOREWORD

Cindy Wimmer's bold work and strong personal style drew my attention several years ago after seeing so many of her stunning designs in various wireworking magazines. Then I won a blog contest she hosted—the prize was a double-heart pendant of copper and bronze, stamped "joy." So simple, and yet the detail and perfect technique evident in the piece made it one of my favorites. After that, Cindy and I talked online and shared ideas: our friendship was born.

At about the same time we met, I had begun working in polymer clay and was making lots of beads as I experimented with different techniques. Cindy was the first wire artist I met who enthusiastically embraced my medium. In the course of our frequent jewelry collaborations, she worked her wire magic with many of my polymer beads and even included them in one of her projects for *Wire Style 2*. Just as she saw the design possibilities for using polymer in her designs, I discovered what a huge difference handmade wire links made in my necklaces, earrings, and bracelets. I no longer had to dilute my designs with bland commercial findings. And I had a large vocabulary of wire designs with which to craft chains, earring findings, bracelet charms, and even bails for focal elements. I started using wire links in everything I made.

I'm thrilled that Cindy is sharing her latest designs and ideas with the wider world in *The Missing Link*. Whether you already work in wire; are someone who beads or makes jewelry; are a mixed-media enthusiast; or are an artist working in polymer clay, ceramic, or lampwork—this book will transform your finished designs. In fact, you might find that the links you'll learn to make in this book will become the actual starting point for a design or even inspire a whole new style of working.

I'm honored to write this foreword. I respect Cindy, her devotion to her art, and the way she lives in the world with integrity, gentleness, and strength. Her friendship means a lot to me. I'm so impressed with the work she's presented in this book. I think you'll turn to it often for inspiration and for ideas to spark your own jewelry designs.

Christine Damm,
polymer clay jewelry artist

INTRODUCTION

The wire link as a functional component is at the heart of handcrafted jewelry. Whether you are an accomplished designer or just starting your adventure in wireworking, *The Missing Link* will introduce you to how wire links can enhance your jewelry designs.

My first forays into jewelry fabrication began with wire seven years ago, and wire is still the central element in my designs today. It didn't take long for me to realize that working with wire is like a long country road with many interesting forks. There is always a new way to work with wire, a new twist, a new way to incorporate it into your work.

Calling attention to the wire link as an important element in its own right pays tribute to wire's boundless possibilities. I'm excited to share with you thirty original wire link projects and fifteen creative jewelry projects that include one or more of those links. Wire links are relevant to *any* jewelry medium, from stringing to metalwork and everything in between!

Like many of you, my interest in crafting and creating can be traced back to a beloved family member—my grandmother. She took great pride in her handiwork and instilled in me a deep respect for the handmade. Guided by her exacting principles, I have written this book with detailed information on wire fundamentals, along with essential tools and techniques. You will learn how to make a wide range of wire links successfully through instructions that are accompanied by step-by-step photos. After you have enjoyed mastering each of these links (or maybe even sooner), you can test-drive the links in complete jewelry projects. This final collection by accomplished jewelry designers demonstrates the versatility and functionality of wire links as connectors, focals, chain, and decorative elements in your jewelry designs.

If you didn't realize all of the potential waiting for you within a single wire link, I hope that *The Missing Link* will help you see those pieces of wire in a whole new way!

WIRE ESSENTIALS

Wire comes in an array of metals, hardnesses, and shapes. How do you know what type of wire to choose for your project? Here you'll find an overview to familiarize you with the various types of wire used in this book and their pros and cons. No two types of wire will feel the same when you work with them; experiment and practice to get a feel for the different types of wire and to discover which one is most suited to your design style. The best way to learn is simply through trial and error. Buy a big roll of copper wire and get started. Confidence and creative freedom will follow!

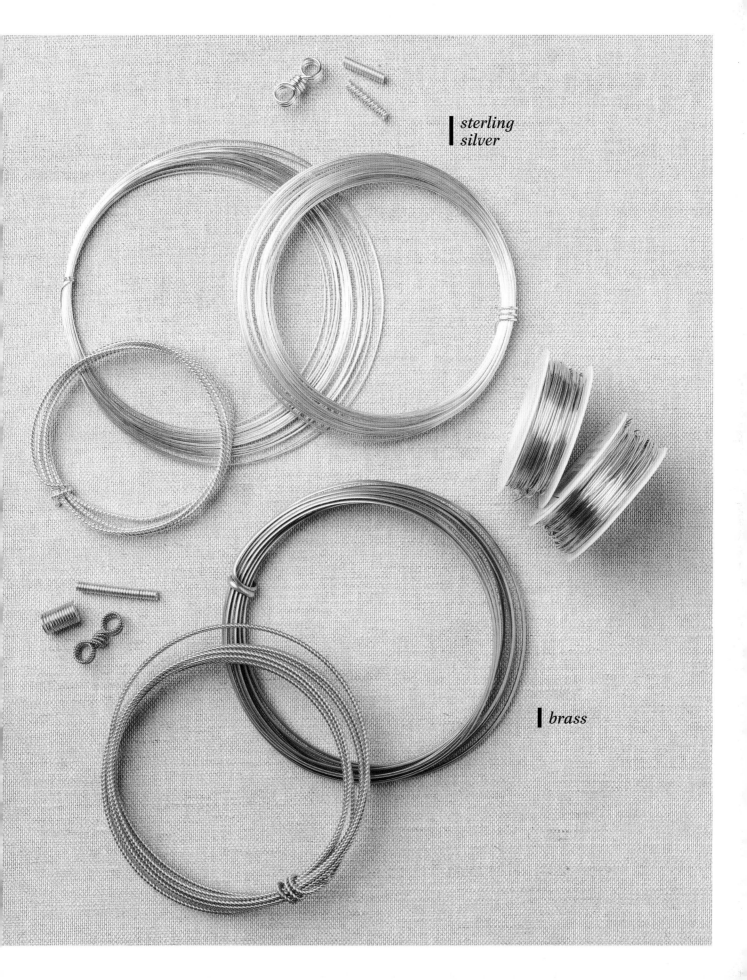

*sterling
silver*

brass

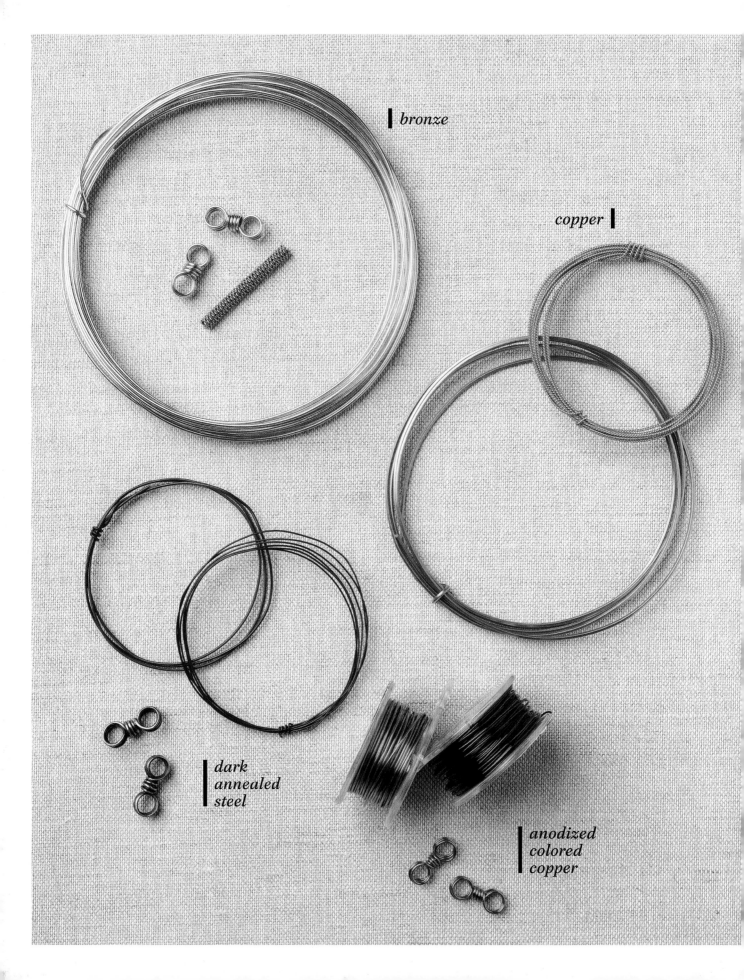

bronze

copper

*dark
annealed
steel*

*anodized
colored
copper*

Gauge and Hardness

Wire is available in various sizes, or diameters. "Gauge" is a term that refers to wire's thickness. The lower the gauge number, the thicker and heavier the wire. Heavy- to medium-gauge wire, such as 12- to 18-gauge, is used to make jump rings, clasps, and to make strong foundations for wire links. Finer gauge wire, such as 20- through 24-gauge, is too thin for structural work but great for coiling, wrapping, and other decorative treatments.

Wire temper, or hardness, refers to the malleability level of a wire. Wire is offered in three hardnesses: dead-soft, half-hard, and full-hard. Wire becomes stiffer as you work with it; this is called "work-hardening." A single piece of wire can go from dead-soft to full-hard temper as it is worked. Dead-soft wire is very pliable and is a popular choice for wireworkers. However, it needs to be hardened to maintain its shape. I prefer to work with dead-soft wire in gauges up to 18-gauge. Half-hard wire is slightly stiffer and holds a shape well, such as angles. I use half-hard wire when working with 20-gauge and higher. Full-hard wire is very rigid, and I have not had a need to work with it for making wire links. You'll find that you'll develop your own preferences for wire hardness the more you work with wire.

Metals

STERLING SILVER. Sterling silver is an all-around favorite choice for wire. Sterling silver is an alloy containing at least 92.5 percent silver. The remaining 7.5 percent is another metal, usually copper. This composition makes sterling silver easy to shape and ensures a beautiful patina. Although sterling silver is ideal to work with, its rising cost has led many jewelry designers to consider alternative metals.

SILVER-FILLED. This wire offers the appearance of sterling silver at a more affordable price. A layer of sterling silver is bonded to a brass wire core. The thickness of the silver overlay is measured by its overall weight, either 1/20 or 1/10 (the thicker and more expensive choice). Silver-filled wire is stiffer to manipulate than sterling silver.

COPPER. Copper wire is readily available, inexpensive, and malleable, making it an ideal practice wire. I practice making all of my wire links in copper wire first. Copper is a popular choice for finished jewelry as well. I prefer to use raw copper wire, sometimes referred to as "bare" copper wire. It oxidizes naturally and with patina solutions. Bear in mind, the copper sold in craft stores is often coated and will remain shiny. Check the descriptive information on the package carefully if you plan to oxidize the wire later. To maintain a patina, some choose to apply a sealant to their copper jewelry. Frequently, the best place to purchase copper wire is your local hardware store.

BRASS. Brass wire is an alloy of copper and zinc; the percentage varies by manufacturer. Red brass, also known as "rich low brass" or jeweler's bronze, is an alloy of 85 percent copper and 15 percent zinc. Its pinkish hue is due to its higher copper content. Yellow brass has higher zinc content—usually 30 percent zinc—and therefore has a bright yellow color compared to the pinkish tone of red brass. Brass is an economical substitute for gold-filled wire. However, it is noticeably stiffer than silver or copper wire. Brass takes on a rich, warm patina. Liver of sulfur, the most popular agent for oxidizing metal, does not provide consistent results with brass, so I have recommended alternatives in the materials lists that accompany the projects.

BRONZE. Bronze wire, also known as phosphor bronze, is a copper and tin alloy. Bronze wire is not quite yellow like brass or as red as copper. Be careful to purchase true bronze wire and not bronze-colored wire. Bronze wire tarnishes naturally and oxidizes well with liver of sulfur or other agents. Although bronze wire is available in a dead-soft hardness, it, too, is not as flexible as sterling silver or copper wire.

DARK ANNEALED STEEL. Dark annealed steel wire is an affordable wire that can be found in the hardware store easily. It is covered in a black carbon coating but can be cleaned with steel wool or fine sandpaper. Annealed steel wire can be an alternative to choose when you want the look of oxidized silver wire, without the expense. Steel wire is stiff and must be cut with heavy-duty wire cutters (your regular jewelry-making cutters will be damaged if you use them). When this wire gets wet, it rusts. To protect steel wire components from rusting, I recommend applying a microcrystalline wax or acrylic-based spray as a protective sealant.

ANODIZED COLORED COPPER. Colored copper wire is made of pure copper wire with a permanently colored nontarnish coating. A wide range of colors is available allowing your creativity to truly take flight. Take care when working with colored copper wire as its nylon finish is durable but can be scratched.

gauge	round	half-round	square
2g	●	◗	■
3g	●	◗	■
4g	●	◗	■
6g	●	◗	■
7g	●	◗	■
8g	●	◗	■
9g	●	◗	■
10g	●	◗	■
11g	●	◗	■
12g	●	◗	■
13g	●	◗	■
14g	●	◗	■
16g	●	◗	■
18g	●	◗	■
19g	•	◗	■
20g	•	·	■
21g	•	·	·
22g	•	·	·
24g	·	·	·
26g	·	·	·

Shape

When selecting the right wire for your project, don't forget to consider all of the wire shapes that are available! Round wire is the most familiar shape, but other shapes to consider are half-round, square, twisted, and patterned wire. There are pros and cons for each shape, and you'll discover your favorites as you experiment. For example, square wire can add interesting angles to a design. However, it can be challenging to keep this four-sided wire "on the square" when you wrap it so you don't introduce unintentional twists.

Try your hand working with all of these wire shapes with the projects in this book.

TOOLS OF THE TRADE

One of the great things about working with wire is that only a handful of tools are needed to make something amazing. You can pack up your essential tools and a spool of wire and bring your studio with you room to room, or out the door. The tools I find essential for getting started are round-nose pliers, chain-nose pliers, flat-nose pliers, and flush cutters. Buy what you can afford, but consider investing in good-quality tools as soon as you are able; you will feel the difference.

As you continue working with wire, you'll discover many additional tools to add to your foundation. Add these tools as you need them and see how they can help you create beautiful designs and make doing so easier all the while.

ROUND-NOSE PLIERS. Round-nose pliers are a fundamental tool in a wireworker's arsenal. Round-nose pliers have two pointed and tapered round jaws. These pliers are used to form jump rings, loops, and spirals of various sizes. It is helpful to have both the standard-sized round-nose pliers and long round-nose pliers on hand. Long round-nose pliers have a larger diameter barrel, which is very useful when you wish to make larger jump rings and loops.

FLAT-NOSE PLIERS. Flat-nose pliers have straight sides and top edge, perfect for making sharp, clean bends in wire. They can also be used to hold wire when creating spirals or, with a second pair of pliers, to open jump rings. Wire can be straightened with these pliers as well.

CHAIN-NOSE PLIERS. Chain-nose pliers are tapered with a flat inner jaw. These pliers can be used to hold wire, bend wire, open and close jump rings, and to tuck in ends of wire in tight spaces.

FLUSH CUTTERS. Flush cutters are a necessity for wirework, and investing in high-quality cutters will serve you well. These cutters have jaws that are angled on one side and flat on the other. A variety of flush cutters are available, with smaller tips for a close cut to heavy-duty flush cutters (see page 16) that are useful for thicker wire up to 8-gauge.

STEPPED PLIERS AND BAIL-FORMING PLIERS. Stepped pliers have round barrels that increase in diameter with each step, giving you several sizes of mandrels in one tool. Bail-forming pliers have non-graduated barrels in two diameters.

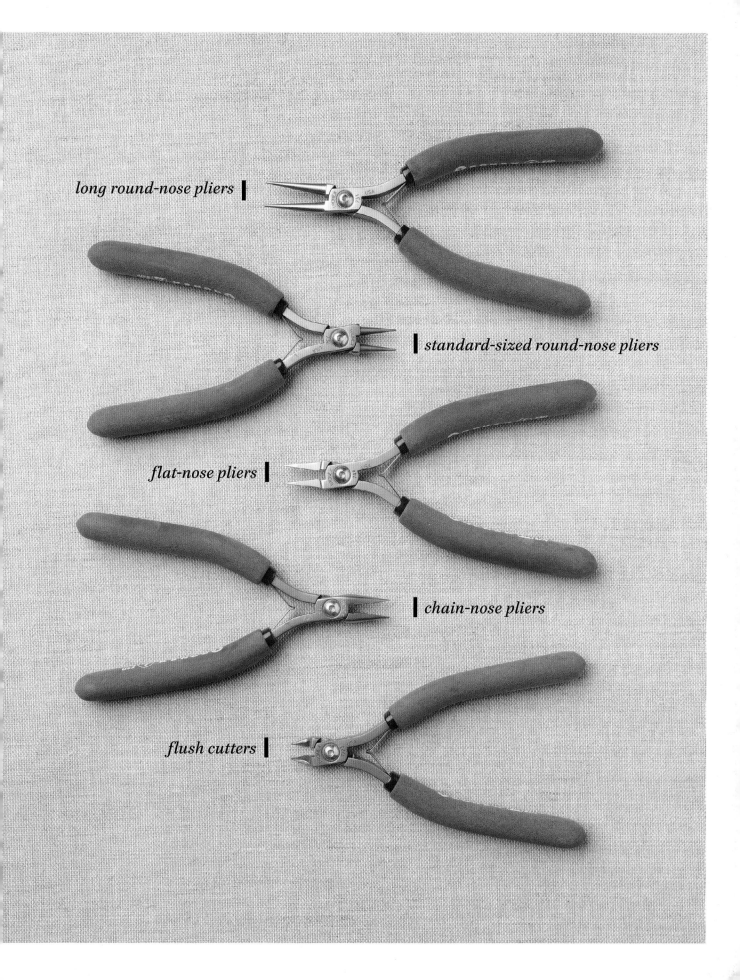

long round-nose pliers

standard-sized round-nose pliers

flat-nose pliers

chain-nose pliers

flush cutters

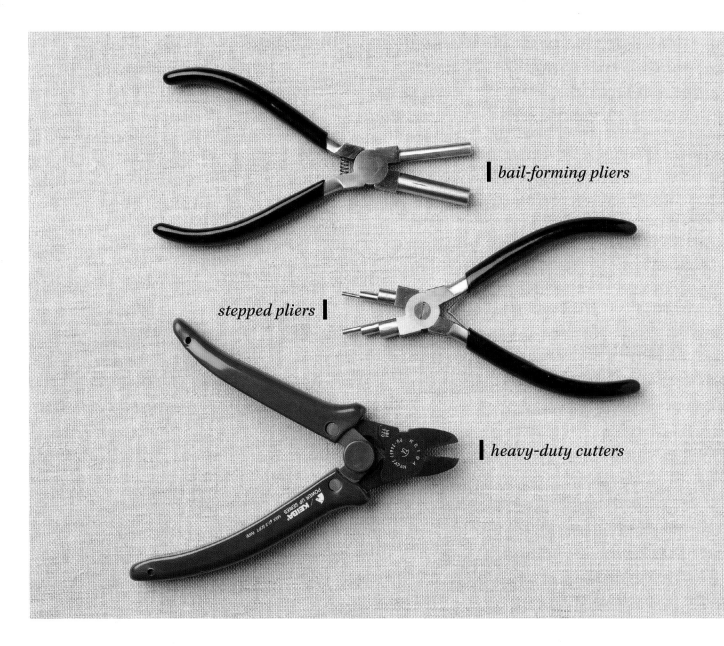

bail-forming pliers

stepped pliers

heavy-duty cutters

With these pliers on hand, you can easily bend and form loops and create coils and jump rings in a variety of sizes. In this book, the barrel sizes for my stepped pliers are 2 mm, 2.5 mm, 3.5 mm, 5 mm, 7 mm, and 8 mm. And the barrel sizes for my bail-forming pliers are 6 mm and 8.5 mm.

RAWHIDE AND PLASTIC MALLETS.
These mallets have a somewhat soft surface and are used to work-harden wire without marring and changing its shape.

CHASING HAMMER.
Chasing hammers are used with the bench block to forge (flatten and shape) wire. Technically, a goldsmith's hammer is the correct tool for flattening wire. I favor the chasing hammer, however, because its surface is slightly domed on one side and does not dent the wire when hammering. This side can be used to flatten and work-harden wire. The ball end can be used to add indentations and texture to the wire.

BRASS STAMPING HAMMER.
One- or two-pound brass hammers are used to strike **DESIGN STAMPS** (see page 18) to make a strong impression on wire and metal.

FILES.
Flat files are used to smooth the sharp ends of wire. Half-round files are used to file curved surfaces, the inside of rings, and corners. These two types of files are essential to have on hand and may be the only ones you will need for working with wire. Filing is always done in one direction.

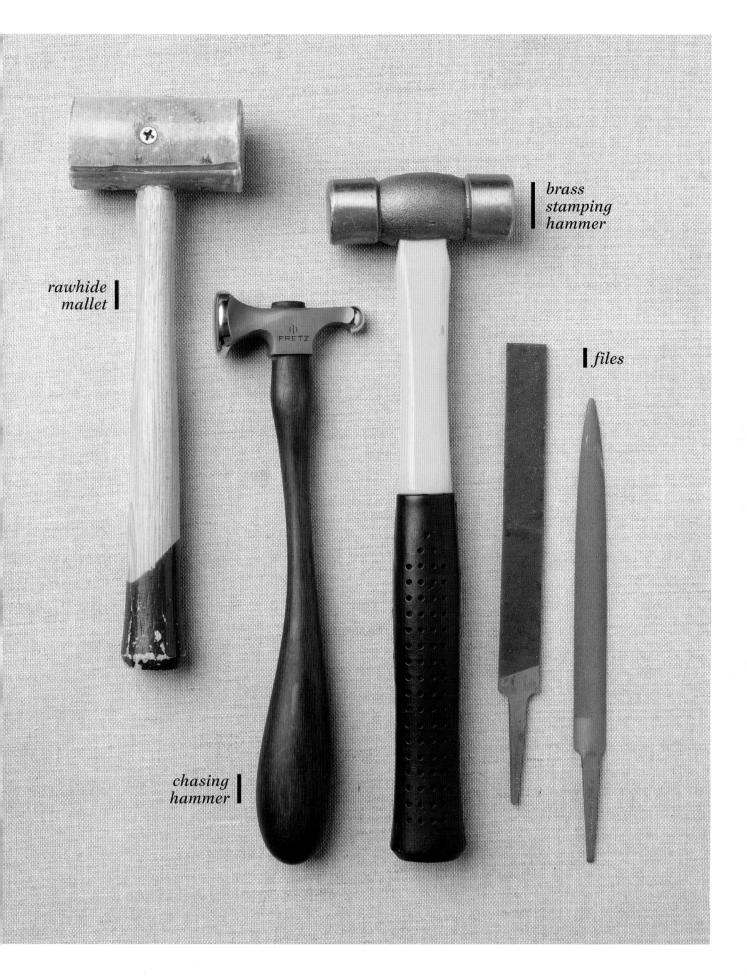

rawhide mallet

brass stamping hammer

files

chasing hammer

leather sandbag

design stamps

polishing cloths

two-hole screw-down punch

steel bench block

steel wool

patina

metal darkener

liver of sulfur gel

STEEL BENCH BLOCK. Made of solid steel, the bench block provides a smooth, flat surface for hammering. The block can be used when adding texture and work-hardening wire as well. To minimize noise and cushion the impact of hammer blows, I use a specially made **LEATHER SAND-BAG** (rubber works well, too). Note: If the surface of your steel bench block is scratched, those marks will transfer to your metal.

TWO-HOLE SCREW-DOWN PUNCH. This handy tool easily punches holes in soft metal. With screw-down levers, you can punch both 1.6 mm and 2.3 mm holes. Just mark the spot with a Sharpie and punch. Hole-punch pliers can be used instead.

STEEL WOOL AND POLISHING CLOTHS. Superfine steel wool (#0000) is indispensable for both cleaning wire and for polishing wire components that have been oxidized. Steel wool removes excess oxidization from the surface of metal, while any grooves will remain darkened. Polishing cloths are then used to add final shine. You can skip polishing with a cloth if the piece is going to be placed in the tumbler.

OXIDIZING SOLUTIONS. Liver of sulfur is a popular choice for adding patina to silver and copper wire. Liver of sulfur (LOS) comes in several forms, such as liquid, chunks, and gel. The gel form is my favorite for ease of use and longer shelf life. Other chemical solutions for adding patina to metal include those under the brand names Black Max, Silver Max, JAX, and Novacan Black Patina for solder, among others. Brass darkening solutions specifically for brass are also available.

deluxe coiling tool with a
variety of mandrel sizes

basic
coiling
tool

tumbler and
stainless-steel shot

variety of mandrels,
including Sharpie or pen

COILING TOOL. You can create wire coils by hand by winding wire around a mandrel. However, I prefer to use a coiling tool, which allows you to create a tight coil in far less time than winding by hand. You can work with a very simple coiling tool that produces uniform coils or choose a more deluxe coiling tool that has several sizes of mandrels. Both versions are also perfect for making your own jump rings.

MANDRELS. Mandrels are used to wrap wire around to shape wire or create coils and jump rings. Alternatively, you can use tools you have handy, such as a Sharpie pen, a coiling tool, or stepped or bail-forming pliers. The punches of a metal dapping set make handy mandrels, too, and offer a large range of sizes.

TUMBLER. You'll be glad you invested in a rotary tumbler. It is designed for work-hardening, cleaning, and polishing metal. It can also soften tool marks on your wire pieces. Mixed stainless-steel shot, water, and a burnishing compound or non-ultra liquid dish soap are added to the barrel of the tumbler, along with wire components or finished jewelry.

A rotary tumbler filled with mixed stainless-steel shot is my go-to for work-hardening links.

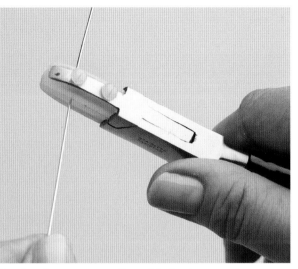

If preferred, you can use pliers with plastic-covered jaws to straighten wire.

TECHNIQUES

I remember when I first learned how to make a wrapped loop, sitting in a class of three at my local crafts store. Working carefully, I added a bead and made one wrapped loop after another until a bracelet was formed. When I tried on my finished bracelet, I knew then that a door was opening to something wonderful—from that time forward I have remained absolutely hooked on working with wire. Do you remember the excitement you felt when you learned a new technique for the very first time?

Here are the most frequently used techniques for working with wire. Use this as a refresher if you're already an old hand at working with wire. If you are just getting started, please be assured that new doors will be opened for you once you master these techniques.

Cleaning, Cutting, and Straightening Wire

Here are a few basic techniques to implement when working with wire:

◆ Clean your wire before you begin any wireworking. Pull the wire through a small ball of #0000 steel wool or a polishing cloth. This process will remove dirt and will also help to straighten the wire.

◆ To straighten wire, I've never found it necessary to use a special straightening tool (large pliers with plastic-covered jaws). Simply pull the wire through a polishing cloth or through your fingertips. You can also lightly tap on the bent wire with a rawhide mallet on the bench block. If the wire is kinked, carefully squeeze the wire in the jaws of the chain-nose or flat-nose pliers and press down to straighten.

◆ Begin your wire projects with a flush-cut end. Place the flat edge of the cutters against the usable end of the wire to make a cut. There should then be a flush end to the piece of wire. If desired, you can smooth the cut end further with a few passes of a flat file.

◆ Keep the famous carpenter's maxim in mind: Measure twice and cut once. When you are using precious metals such as sterling silver, this is especially important to observe. In general, however, it is better to cut a wire too long and have ample wire to work with rather than to come up short and have to recut a piece of wire. It can be very frustrating to restart a piece when you come up just a fraction too short.

◆ As you become more comfortable working with wire, you will likely prefer to "work from the spool" rather than cut predetermined lengths of wire. You will eliminate a considerable amount of wire waste this way.

Simple Loop

Simple loops open like jump rings and make linking components easy. If possible, use a heavier gauge wire when incorporating simple loops so that the finished piece is sturdy and won't be pulled open easily.

1 Flush-cut and file the end of the wire. Grasp one end of the wire with the back of the round-nose pliers (**FIG. 1**).

2 Roll the wire forward as far as possible. Remove the pliers and reinsert, rolling forward to form a complete loop (**FIG. 2**).

3 Use chain-nose pliers to grasp the inside of the loop at the base. Bend back your wrist, centering the loop over the straight part of the wire like a lollipop (**FIG. 3**).

4 If necessary, reinsert the round-nose pliers into the loop, positioning it so the loop is perpendicular to the tail wire.

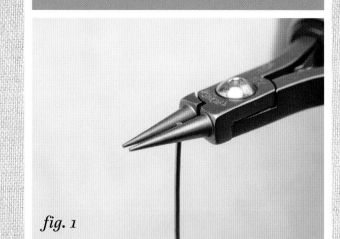

fig. 1

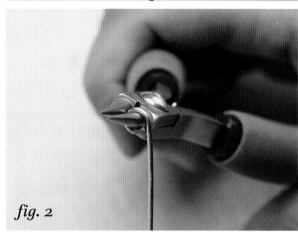

fig. 2

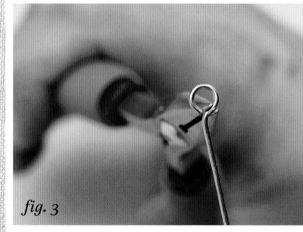

fig. 3

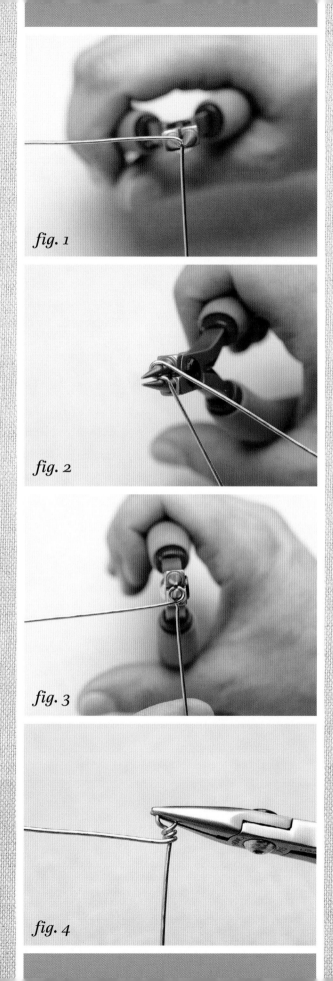

fig. 1

fig. 2

fig. 3

fig. 4

Wrapped Loop

Wrapping loops is a fundamental technique in wirework. One wrapped loop will lead to another, putting you well on your way to making wire jewelry that lasts.

1 Hold the wire at least 2" (5 cm) from one end with round-nose pliers. Make a 90° bend (**FIG. 1**).

2 Grasp the bend in the wire with round-nose pliers. Using your hand, bring the wire tail up and around the top of the pliers so that the tail now points down (**FIG. 2**).

3 Remove the pliers and reposition the bottom jaw inside the curve. Pull the tail wire tightly around the bottom jaw of the pliers, forming a complete loop. The straight wires will form a 90° angle (**FIG. 3**).

4 Grasp the loop with chain-nose pliers and wrap the tail wire around the straight wire two or three times. Be sure to keep the wires at a 90° angle to keep the wrapping wire straight. Trim the excess tail wire and press the end down with chain-nose pliers (**FIG. 4**).

TIP

It may seem silly, but an easy way to remember these steps is to compare them to building a snowman. First you make his head (the wire loop) and then wrap his scarf (the tail wire) around his neck!

Coiling Wire

Coiled wire can add immediate texture and visual interest to wire designs. Coils really spark my imagination and are one of my favorite techniques. I prefer to use a coiling tool for speed and consistency when I create coils, but they can be made easily with any mandrel on hand. You can coil directly onto wire as well. Coils are also the foundation for making jump rings.

1 Hold the coiling wire against the mandrel with your nondominant hand, leaving a 1" (2.5 cm) tail to hold onto. With your dominant hand, pull the wire up and around the mandrel firmly, keeping the coils close together (**FIG. 1**).

2 Wrap the wire away from your body. Make the wraps parallel to one another by keeping the wire at a 90° angle to the mandrel. It is important to retain your momentum when winding, keeping the wire taut. Compress the wires together with chain-nose pliers if gaps develop (**FIG. 2**).

3 When the coil is the length you desire, remove it from the mandrel. Flush-cut any excess wire at both ends.

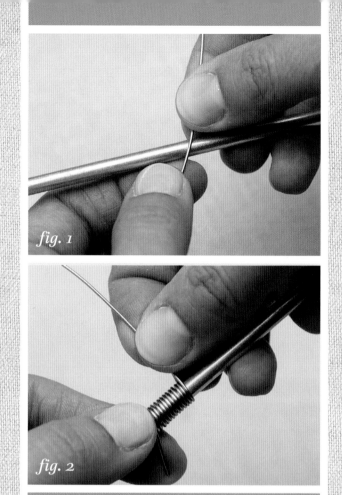

fig. 1

fig. 2

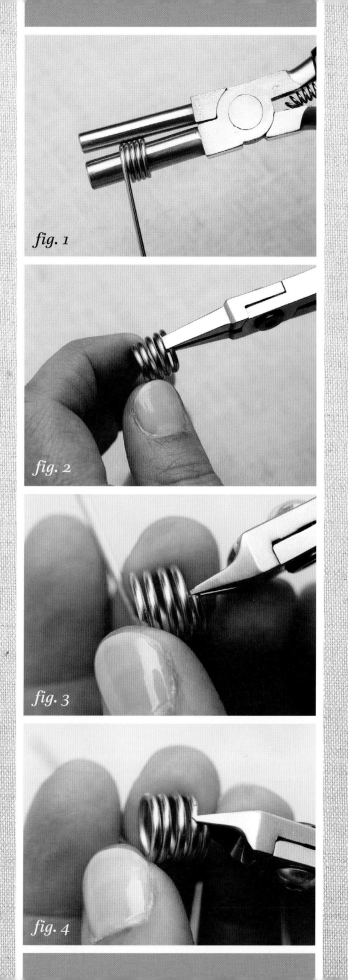

fig. 1

fig. 2

fig. 3

fig. 4

Jump Rings

Making your own jump rings is a cinch and gives you the freedom to customize your wire design. You can use any type of wire and in any diameter you need. If you'll be using the jump ring as a connector, it is important to use a heavier wire gauge. For example, 16-gauge wire will make a sturdy, all-purpose jump ring.

1 Coil a length of wire firmly around a mandrel. Each complete coil will make one jump ring. A coiling mandrel, bail-forming pliers, and even a Sharpie all work well (FIG. 1).

2 Remove the coil from the mandrel and pull the coil apart slightly with your fingers or with flat- or chain-nose pliers (FIG. 2).

3 Flush-cut the ends of the coil (FIG. 3).

4 Turn the cutters over and line them up with the cut just made. Flush-cut perpendicular to the coil to create a single jump ring. This will create a flush cut on both ends of the jump ring (FIG. 4).

5 To create each subsequent jump ring, flush-cut the end of the wire. Flip the cutters over and flush-cut perpendicular to the coil again.

TIP

When using pliers, coil the wire toward the back of the pliers so the finished coil will push out toward the tip of the pliers. This way, you can make a coil of any length, even if the barrel of your pliers is short.

OPENING AND CLOSING JUMP RINGS.

Open and close jump rings properly to prevent distortion of their circular shape.

1 Use chain-nose and flat-nose pliers to grasp each side of the jump ring opening. To open, twist one side toward you and push the other side away (**FIG. 1**).

2 To close the jump ring, bring the ends back together using the pliers. Move the ends back and forth beyond the closed position a few times, easing the ends together so that there is no gap (**FIG. 2**). Work-harden new jump rings by hammering them with a rawhide mallet on a steel bench block. Tumble your jump rings to increase durability.

TIP

When purchasing commercial jump rings, you'll notice that the rings are often measured by their diameters. ID refers to inner diameter, and OD refers to outer diameter.

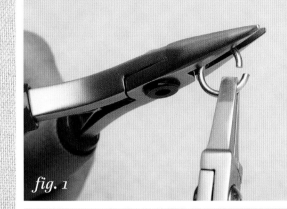

fig. 1

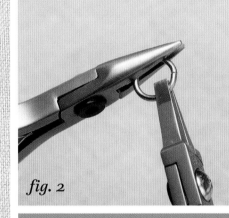

fig. 2

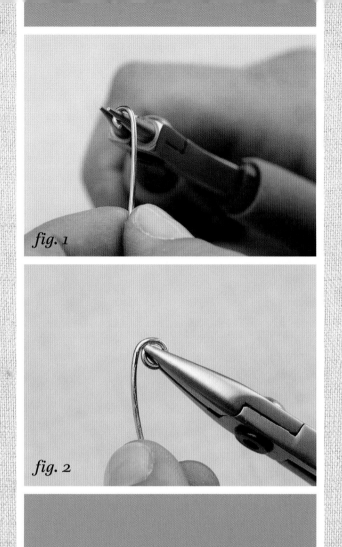

fig. 1

fig. 2

Spirals

Spirals have long been studied in nature, have many symbolic meanings, and are a classic when it comes to working with wire as well. To maintain a spiral shape, use a heavier gauge of wire.

1 Flush-cut one end of the wire. Grasp the end of the wire with the tip of the round-nose pliers. Roll the wire away from you with one hand while pushing the tail wire against the pliers with the thumb of your other hand to form a small simple loop (**FIG. 1**).

2 Before closing the loop completely, switch to the flat-nose pliers. Hold the loop with the flat-nose pliers and begin winding the tail wire around the loop. Continue winding the wire with your thumb, moving in small increments to form a spiral. Continue until the desired spiral size is reached (**FIG. 2**).

TIP

Forming a round-shaped loop in the first step is essential to create a nice, round spiral. It is helpful to flatten the tip of the wire with a chasing hammer on the bench block before starting a spiral. The tapered tip of wire will be easier to shape into a circle, especially if you are using a thick gauge of wire.

Wire Clasps

S-CLASP. Flush-cut the ends of a
3¼" (8.5 cm) piece of 16-gauge wire.
Flatten the ends with a chasing hammer on a bench block. Grasp the end
of the wire with the tip of round-nose
pliers. Roll the wire forward to create
simple loops on each end of the wire
that face opposite directions (**FIG. 1**).
Grasp the wire just under the loop with
the wide end of one plier jaw or the
8.5 mm barrel of bail-forming pliers.
Roll the wire forward until it forms a
hook shape (**FIG. 2**). Repeat on the
opposite end of the wire (**FIG. 3**).
Leave one hook open slightly so that it
can be hooked onto a jump ring or the
eye of the clasp. Flatten the curves of
the clasp on both sides with a chasing
hammer on a bench block.

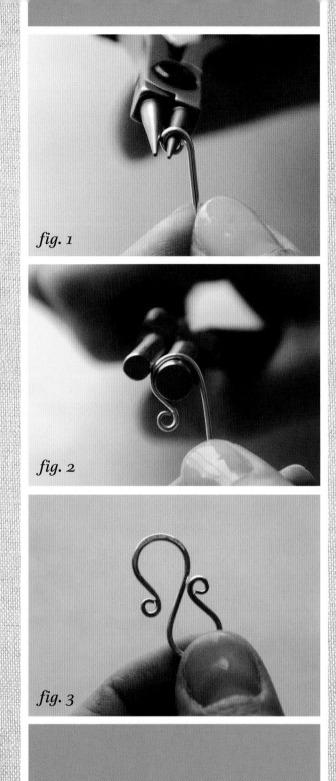

fig. 1

fig. 2

fig. 3

fig. 1

fig. 2

fig. 3

fig. 1

HOOK CLASP. Create a double hook clasp using 4" (10 cm) of 18-gauge wire. Bend the wire in half and press the bend tightly with chain-nose pliers (**FIG. 1**). Flush-cut the wire ends. Grasp both cut ends in the back of the round-nose pliers and roll the pliers forward to form simple loops (**FIG. 2**). Grasp the bent end with the 8.5 mm barrel of the bail-forming pliers and roll the pliers forward to shape the hook (**FIG. 3**).

Work-Hardening

Work-hardening is an important concept to be familiar with as a wireworker. When you bend, hammer, and coil wire, you are work-hardening the wire. Technically speaking, the molecules in the wire are being moved and pressed closer together, causing the wire to become increasingly stiff. If wire becomes too stiff, it can eventually break under pressure.

To work-harden a specific portion of a wire link, such as a simple loop, use a rawhide or nylon mallet and a steel bench block. Place the link on the bench block and firmly strike with the mallet multiple times (**FIG. 1**). Make sure your bench block is free from scratches; otherwise, the marks will transfer to your wire. A rotary tumbler with mixed stainless-steel shot is also extremely useful for work-hardening wire links, especially groups at a time.

Finishing

OXIDIZING SOLUTIONS

You can give your finished jewelry a darkened, antiqued look by oxidizing it. This is purely optional and a matter of personal preference. As for me, I almost always choose to oxidize my jewelry. It accentuates the details that are in relief and adds incredible visual depth to wirework when the high points are polished. There are many methods to achieve an aged look for your metal without having to wait for natural oxidization to occur. Some of the many ways to explore oxidizing include fuming, heat treatment, and a natural method that uses hard-cooked eggs. In this book, however, we will be using liver of sulfur and commercial patinas that are readily available and produce consistent results.

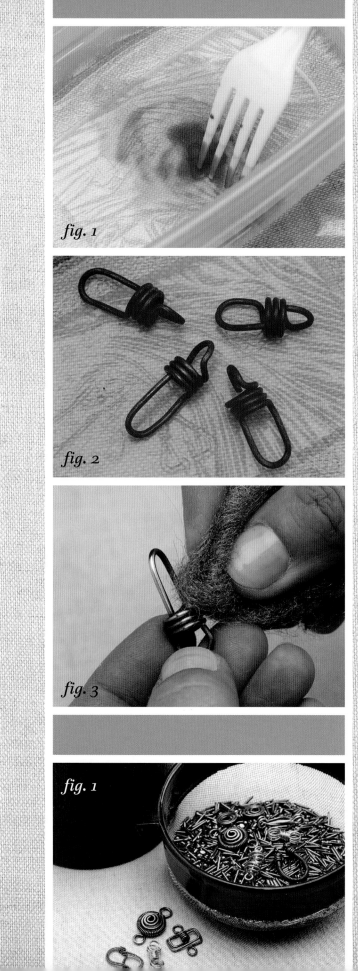

fig. 1

fig. 2

fig. 3

fig. 1

TIPS

When working with oxidizing agents, consider safety first. Wear plastic gloves and work in a well-ventilated area inside or outdoors because the fumes may be harmful.

Be sure your components are free of dirt and residual oils before oxidizing.

LIVER OF SULFUR (LOS).
This is by far the most popular choice for antiquing sterling and silver-filled, copper, and bronze wires. It can be purchased in rock, liquid, and gel forms. I prefer the gel form because

it's easy to use and has an extremely long shelf life. Keep everything you need handy in a plastic shoe box: a plastic bowl reserved just for oxidizing, plastic fork or tongs, the container of LOS gel, a box of baking soda, and plastic gloves.

1 Pour a cup or so of very warm (but not boiling) water into the bowl. Dip the fork into the LOS gel and swirl the fork around in the water to dissolve. I like to use a fork so that it can also be used to move the jewelry (**FIG. 1**).

2 Place your wire pieces into the solution until darkened (**FIG. 2**). You can also run your pieces under hot water before adding them to the LOS to hasten the process. The pieces may turn dark quickly or they may take several minutes.

3 Remove the pieces from the solution and rinse under cold water.

4 To dispose of the LOS safely, add a tablespoon of baking soda to neutralize it, then pour it down the drain.

5 Use superfine (#0000) steel wool to buff off any excess oxidization (**FIG. 3**). The inner coils and other recessed areas will remain dark, while the flat and raised areas will shine. Be sure to rinse the piece well afterward to remove any trapped bits of steel wool. Finally, polish the pieces with a polishing cloth or tumble in the rotary tumbler with mixed stainless-steel shot.

CHEMICAL OXIDIZING AGENTS.

There are solutions available that give immediate results without having to be mixed with water. Some of the commonly used brands include Novacan Black Patina, Black Max, Silver Black, and the JAX patinas. They work great if you want to darken a small area or a single component quickly.

To oxidize with one of these agents, wear gloves to hold your component. Dip a dedicated paintbrush or cotton swab into the oxidizing agent and brush onto the area to be oxidized. Alternatively, you can pour a small amount of solution into a small bowl and add the component to it directly. Rinse with cold water. Buff the component with steel wool and a polishing cloth to remove any excess oxidization.

TUMBLING

My most indispensable tool in the studio is my rotary tumbler. It's an optional tool, but a high-quality rotary tumbler is a worthwhile investment if you plan to work with metal. Tumbling your wire components will shine and clean them, help to soften tool marks, and will also help work-harden them. Doesn't that sound wonderful?

I'll admit that when I first bought it, I let my tumbler sit in the box for a few months, feeling a little intimidated by this new electrical piece of equipment. I soon realized that you can hardly go wrong using one: it has been a hardworking studio staple ever since. The steps for tumbling are easy:

1 Fill the barrel with 1 to 2 pounds (454 to 907 g) of mixed stainless-steel shot. The exact amount is not critical but more of a preference. Add the wire components or jewelry. Add 1 or 2 drops of mild non-ultra dishwashing liquid or burnishing compound. Fill the barrel with water that is about 1" (2.5 cm) above the jewelry.

2 Leave the pieces in the tumbler anywhere from a half hour on, depending on the materials used in the jewelry. If tumbling all-metal components, such as wire links or clasps, I will oftentimes leave them in the tumbler for an hour or more.

3 Pour the contents of the tumbler into a strainer. I like to place the strainer in a bowl to catch any shot that falls through. Rinse the items in the strainer and remove your pieces. Spread stainless-steel shot on paper towels or a dishcloth to dry before returning it to the barrel for storage (**FIG. 1**).

NOW STARRING: THE WIRE LINKS

Here you will find a collection of thirty wire links to spark your imagination. Coil, twist, bend, and experiment with detailed step-by-step directions. No matter what your skill level, you'll learn how to make wire links that will enhance your jewelry designs.

MATERIALS
6" (15 cm) of 16-gauge pure copper
wire

TOOLS
Flat-nose pliers

Stepped pliers or steel mandrel, 2 mm

Flush cutters

Rawhide mallet

Steel bench block

Sharpie

Liver of sulfur

Steel wool, #0000

Rotary tumbler with mixed stainless-
steel shot

Ruler

FINISHED SIZE
¾" × 1½" (1.9 × 3.8 cm)

LEVEL OF DIFFICULTY
Easy ●○○

TIP

*Because this link has
open ends like a jump
ring, it is best to make it
with heavier gauge wire
only and to work-harden
it after forming with a
rawhide mallet or
a tumbler.*

BOW-TIE

Start with a coil and add a few bends to create
a link with angles.

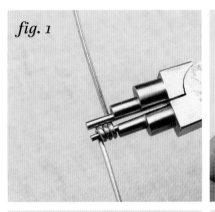

fig. 1

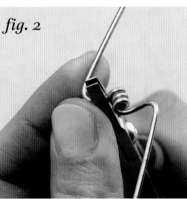

fig. 2

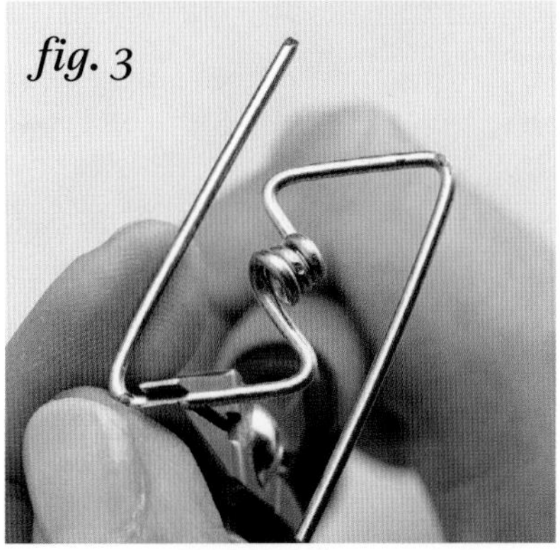

fig. 3

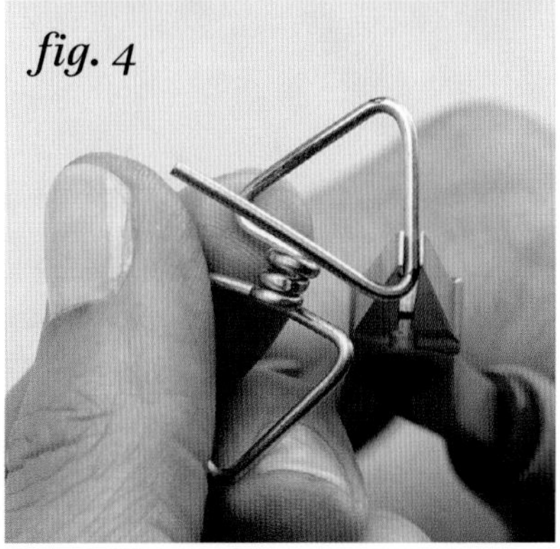

fig. 4

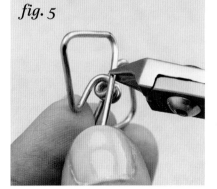

fig. 5

2 Hold the wire horizontally. Grasp
one end of the wire against the coil
with flat-nose pliers. Bend the wire
up against the edge of the pliers at
a 60° angle. Flip the link over and
repeat with the opposite tail wire
(**FIG. 2**).

3 Mark one wire ⅝" (1.5 cm) from the
bend with the Sharpie. Grasp the
wire with flat-nose pliers, placing
the outer edge of the pliers on the
mark. Bend the wire up at a 60°
angle. Repeat on the opposite tail
wire, forming what looks like a
pointy "S" (**FIG. 3**).

4 Mark one wire again ⅝" (1.5 cm)
from the last bend. Bend the wire
in toward the coil at the mark.
Cut the wire flush at the coil. With
flat-nose pliers, move the wire back
and forth like a jump ring until
the cut end is snug against the
coil. Repeat on the opposite side
(**FIGS. 4 AND 5**).

5 Work-harden the link with the
rawhide mallet on the bench block.

6 Oxidize the link with liver of sulfur
(see page 30) and buff the excess
oxidation with steel wool. Tumble
to work-harden and polish.

1 Grasp the middle of the 16-gauge
wire with the 2 mm barrel of the
stepped pliers and make a tight
coil (see page 24) that is three
complete turns.

NOTE: The tail wires should point
in opposite directions as shown
(**FIG. 1**).

TIP

Variations of this link can be made by increasing the size of the mandrel and by using simple loops instead of wrapped loops.

CLASSIC HOOP

Wrapped loops or simple loops, large mandrels
or small, this link can be customized easily to suit
your designs.

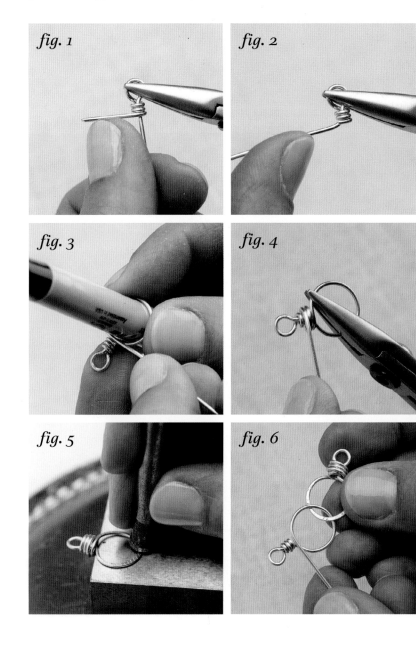

fig. 1

fig. 2

fig. 3

fig. 4

fig. 5

fig. 6

1 Cut 6" (15 cm) of wire and mark the
wire 2" (5 cm) from one end with
the Sharpie. Begin a wrapped loop
(see page 23) at the mark using the
middle of the round-nose pliers,
then wrap the short tail wire around
the longer wire 3 times. Trim the
short tail and pinch in the end with
chain-nose pliers (**FIG. 1**).

2 Grasp the loop with chain-nose
pliers and bend the long wire up
90° (**FIG. 2**).

3 Wrap the wire around the widest
section of the Sharpie to form a
circle (**FIG. 3**).

4 Hold the circle with chain-nose
pliers and wrap the wire around the
previous wraps (**FIG. 4**). Trim the
excess wire.

5 Flatten the circle slightly with the
chasing hammer on the bench
block. If desired, use the brass
stamping hammer and decorative
metal stamps to add surface
designs (**FIG. 5**).

6 Repeat Steps 1 through 3 to create a
second link. Attach the second link
to the first link and then complete
Steps 4 and 5 (**FIG. 6**).

7 Oxidize the link with liver of sulfur
(see page 30) and buff the excess
oxidation with steel wool. Tumble
to work-harden and polish.

MATERIALS

5½" (14 cm) of 16-gauge sterling silver-
filled dead-soft wire

TOOLS

Chain-nose pliers

Round-nose pliers

Stepped pliers, 5 mm

Sharpie (or 12 mm mandrel)

Flush cutters

Flat hand file

Rawhide mallet

Steel bench block

Liver of sulfur

Steel wool, #0000

Rotary tumbler with mixed stainless-
steel shot

Ruler

FINISHED SIZE

½" × ⅞" (1.3 × 2.2 cm)

LEVEL OF DIFFICULTY

Easy ●○○

TIPS

*Tumbling will
also help to soften
any tool marks left from
manipulating the wire loops.*

*Place the link back on the
Sharpie in Step 5 to help
maintain the round shape
while tweaking the
simple loops.*

ENGAGEMENT RING

This romantic link is sure to become a favorite foundation in your jewelry designs. Adapt the mandrel size to suit your project and make consistently beautiful links and chain.

fig. 1

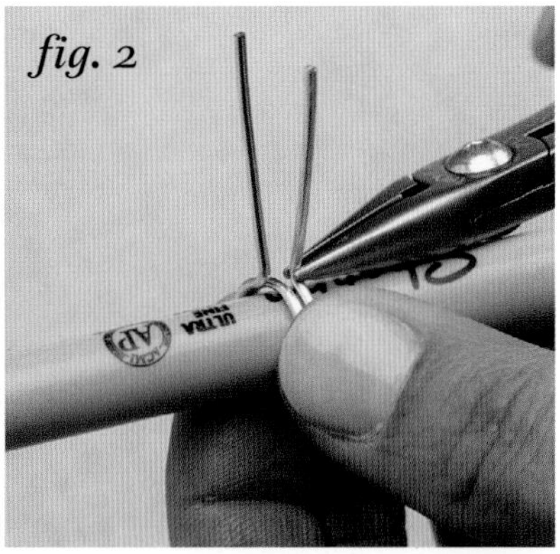

fig. 2

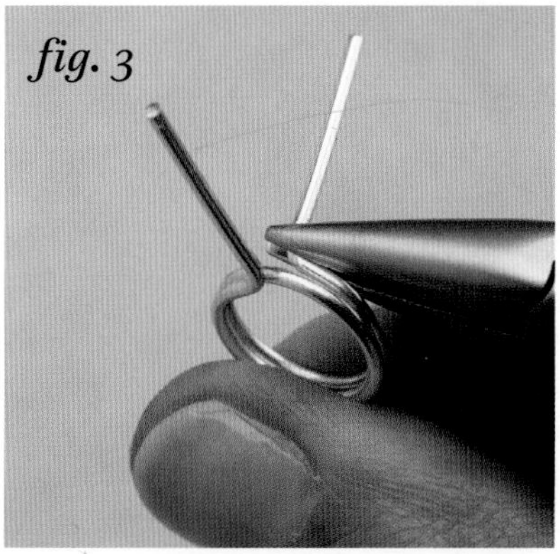

fig. 3

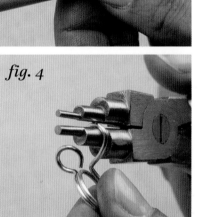

fig. 4

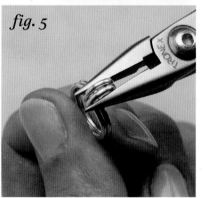

fig. 5

3 Trim each wire tail to ¾" (2 cm) and file smooth. Holding the loops with your fingers, bend each wire tail back 90° with chain-nose pliers (**FIG. 3**).

4 Roll the tip of one wire tail forward using the 5 mm barrel on the stepped pliers, forming a simple loop (see page 22) (**FIG. 4**). Repeat on the other wire tail.

TIP: Forming the second loop will be more difficult with the first loop in the way, so roll it forward as far as possible, then switch to chain-nose pliers and pull the loop forward until it touches the ring.

5 Tweak the simple loops with chain-nose pliers to get them aligned. Squeeze the loops together with the pliers so they are parallel (**FIG. 5**).

6 Hold the simple loops and hammer the larger loops lightly with the rawhide hammer on the bench block to work-harden.

7 Oxidize the link with liver of sulfur (see page 30) and buff the excess oxidation with steel wool. Tumble to work-harden and polish.

1 Center the wire on the Sharpie and wrap both ends of the wire around it, crossing the wires and forming a loop. Wrap the wire twice around the Sharpie, ending with the tails crossing slightly (**FIG. 1**).

2 Keeping the loops on the Sharpie, bend both wire tails to a 90° angle with chain-nose pliers (**FIG. 2**). Remove the Sharpie.

MATERIALS

5½" (14 cm) of 16-gauge sterling silver
  dead-soft wire

TOOLS

Chain-nose pliers

Flat-nose pliers

Bail-forming pliers or steel mandrel,
  6 mm

Flush cutters

Sharpie

Liver of sulfur

Steel wool, #0000

Rotary tumbler with mixed stainless-
  steel shot

Ruler

FINISHED SIZE

⅜" × 1" (.95 × 2.5 cm)

LEVEL OF DIFFICULTY

Easy ●○○

LIGHTBULB

In no time at all, you can create custom chains for your jewelry designs. The simple loop on the Lightbulb link opens and closes like a jump ring, so connecting these links is a snap!

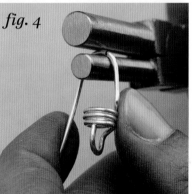

fig. 1

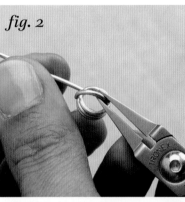

fig. 2

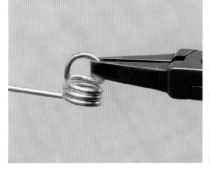

fig. 3

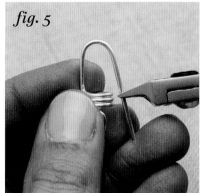

fig. 4

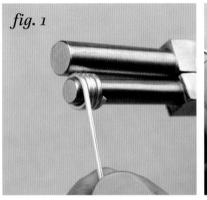

fig. 5

1 Grasp the tip of the wire in the bail-forming pliers and coil (see page 24) it around the 6 mm barrel 4 full turns (**FIG. 1**). Remove the wire.

2 Insert one jaw of the flat-nose pliers under the first coil, with the flat edge lined up with the cut end of the coil. Lift the half coil up so that it is perpendicular to the remaining coils (**FIG. 2**).

3 On the opposite end of the coil, hold the flat-nose pliers perpendicular to the coils. Grasp the tail wire and bend it up 90°. Adjust the tail wire so that it is perpendicular to the half coil (**FIG. 3**).

4 Measure ½" (1.3 cm) from the coil on the tail wire and mark with a Sharpie. Bend the wire at the mark around the 6 mm barrel of the bail-forming pliers (**FIG. 4**).

5 Trim the tail wire with flush cutters so that it overlaps the top coil slightly (**FIG. 5**). Tuck the end of the tail wire into the inside of the coil with flat-nose pliers.

6 Oxidize the link with liver of sulfur (see page 30) and buff the excess oxidation with steel wool. Tumble to work-harden and polish.

TIPS

Wraps can be coiled neatly or wrapped repeatedly over the previous wires for a more organic look.

Using contrasting wires is eye-catching and will yield many different styles!

Any fine-gauge wire can be used in Step 3, from 22- to 26-gauge wire, including twisted wire.

LITTLE ORBITS

Imagine the infinite possibilities when a link begins as a plain wire ring. Mix and match textures and types of wire to create countless combinations of mixed-metal rings.

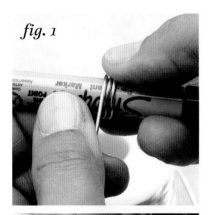

fig. 1

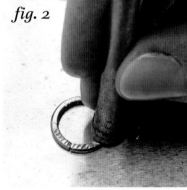

fig. 2

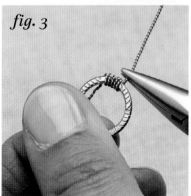

fig. 3

1 Working from the wire spool, wrap the 14-gauge wire around a Sharpie to form a jump ring (see page 25) (**FIG. 1**). Flush-cut the ends of the wire so that the ends meet.

2 Flatten the ring with the chasing hammer on the bench block. If the ring opens from being hammered, reclose the gap with chain- and flat-nose pliers. Hammer with a texturizing hammer or decorative stamps and a brass stamping hammer if desired (**FIG. 2**).

3 Wrap 3" (7.5 cm) of 26-gauge twisted wire around the cut ends of the ring, concealing the split. Continue wrapping the wire around this side of the ring, pulling it tightly with chain-nose pliers (**FIG. 3**). Trim the wire and press down the ends with chain-nose pliers.

4 Repeat Step 3, wrapping 3" (7.5 cm) of round wire around the side of the ring opposite where the first wraps were made.

5 Oxidize the link with liver of sulfur (see page 30) and buff the excess oxidation with steel wool. Tumble to work-harden and polish.

NOTE: If you use brass wire, use Novacan Black or JAX for your oxidizing agent.

TIP

Turn one of the simple loops perpendicular to the link with the flat-nose pliers. It can then be opened and closed like a jump ring and attached to another link to form a chain.

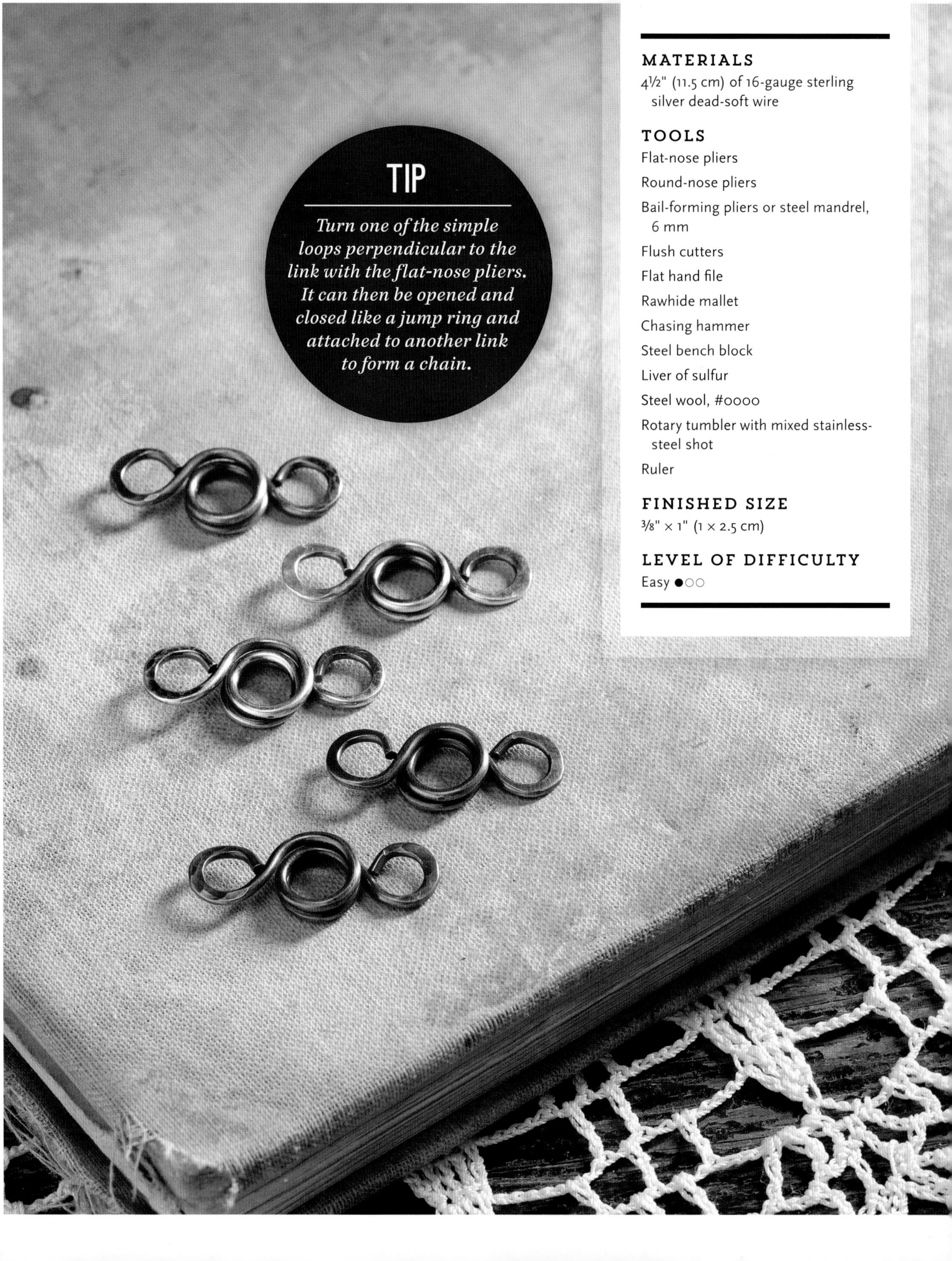

MATERIALS

4½" (11.5 cm) of 16-gauge sterling silver dead-soft wire

TOOLS

Flat-nose pliers

Round-nose pliers

Bail-forming pliers or steel mandrel, 6 mm

Flush cutters

Flat hand file

Rawhide mallet

Chasing hammer

Steel bench block

Liver of sulfur

Steel wool, #0000

Rotary tumbler with mixed stainless-steel shot

Ruler

FINISHED SIZE

⅜" × 1" (1 × 2.5 cm)

LEVEL OF DIFFICULTY

Easy ●○○

LOOPTY LOOP

The Loopty Loop link is so easy to construct and will be a versatile addition to your arsenal of links. Once you make one, you'll want to make another and another!

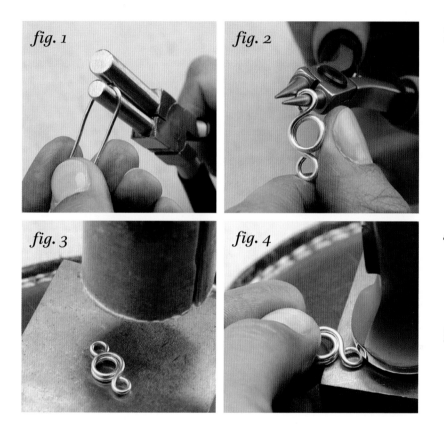

fig. 1

fig. 2

fig. 3

fig. 4

3 Measure ⅝" (1.5 cm) from the middle of the loop and flush-cut one tail wire at that point. File the end smooth. Grasp one end of that tail wire with the back of the round-nose pliers and roll forward, forming a simple loop (see page 22). Repeat with the other tail wire, making sure that the cut ends of the wire are on the same side of the link (**FIG. 2**).

4 Hammer the center loops several times on each side with the rawhide mallet on the bench block. The center loops will spread slightly (**FIG. 3**).

5 Flatten the curves of each simple loop with the chasing hammer on the bench block (**FIG. 4**). Next, hammer the curves on each simple loop with the ball end of the chasing hammer to add texture. Close the simple loops with flat-nose pliers if they open from being hammered.

6 Oxidize the link with liver of sulfur (see page 30) and buff the excess oxidation with steel wool. Tumble to work-harden and polish.

1 Bend the middle of the wire around the 6 mm barrel of the bail-forming pliers, forming a U-shape, with the tails facing downward (**FIG. 1**).

2 Crisscross the wire tightly around the barrel, forming a complete circle (or loop), with the tails facing upward. Crisscross the wire ends around the barrel again, ending with both wires pointing downward. There should be 3 wraps showing around the top side of the barrel and 2 wraps showing on the bottom of the barrel; both tail wires should be pointing downward.

MATERIALS
Spool of 16-gauge pure copper square
   wire, 12½" (31.5 cm) used

TOOLS
Chain-nose pliers

Flat-nose pliers

Round-nose pliers

Stepped pliers or steel mandrels,
   5 mm and 7 mm

Flush cutters

Flat hand file

Chasing hammer

Rawhide mallet

Steel bench block

Sharpie

Liver of sulfur

Steel wool, #0000

Rotary tumbler with mixed stainless-
   steel shot

Ruler

FINISHED SIZE
⅜" × 1¾" (1 × 4.5 cm)

LEVEL OF DIFFICULTY
Easy ●○○

SLIDING RINGS

Add a hint of the unexpected while trying your hand with square wire. The sliding rings add movement to your design and are made with simple jump rings.

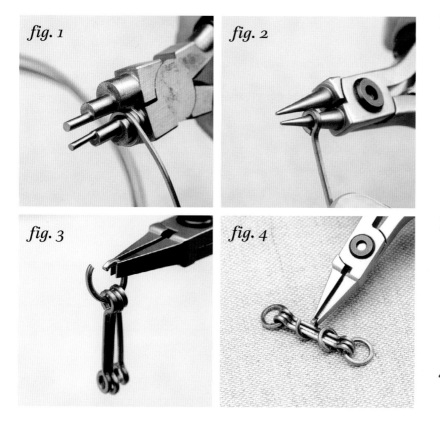

fig. 1

fig. 2

fig. 3

fig. 4

2 Flush-cut three 1¾" (4.5 cm) pieces of wire; file the ends. Make matching marks near the tip of each barrel of the round-nose pliers with a Sharpie, using the marks as a guide to make consistently sized loops. Form a simple loop (see page 22) on both ends of each of the 3 wire pieces, with the openings of the loops on the same side for each piece of wire (**FIG. 2**).

3 Open one of the 7 mm jump rings and attach all 3 loops on one end of the 3 pieces of wire; close the jump ring (**FIG. 3**). Open the second 7 mm jump ring and attach the 3 loops on the other end of the 3 wires; close the jump ring. The wires should be parallel.

4 Open each of the three 5 mm jump rings and close them around the center wires (**FIG. 4**). They should slide loosely on the wires.

5 Oxidize the link with liver of sulfur (see page 30) and buff the excess oxidation with steel wool. Tumble to work-harden and polish.

1 Working from the wire spool, use the 7 mm barrel of the stepped pliers to make 2 jump rings (see page 25) (**FIG. 1**). Make 3 additional jump rings using the 5 mm barrel of the stepped pliers. Close the ends of the jump rings flush and work-harden by hammering several times with the rawhide mallet on the bench block. Set the jump rings aside.

MATERIALS

7" (18 cm) of 18-gauge sterling silver
 dead-soft wire

9" (23 cm) of 22-gauge sterling silver
 half-hard wire

TOOLS

Chain-nose pliers

Flat-nose pliers

Flush cutters

Rawhide mallet

Steel bench block

Sharpie

Liver of sulfur

Steel wool, #0000

Rotary tumbler with mixed stainless-
 steel shot

Ruler

FINISHED SIZE

¾" (2 cm)

LEVEL OF DIFFICULTY

Easy ●○○

TANGLED TRIANGLES

A grapevine-style design takes on a bold new shape! To add contrast to this link, use two different types of wire. For example, a base of 18-gauge copper wrapped with 24-gauge sterling silver twisted wire would look fabulous.

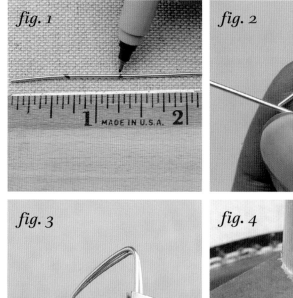

fig. 1

fig. 2

fig. 3

fig. 4

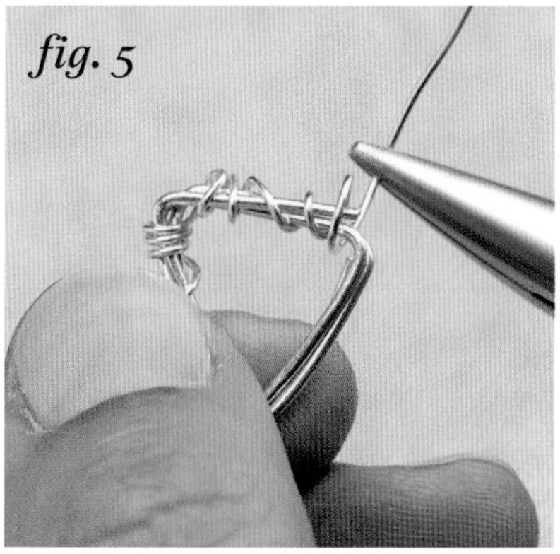

fig. 5

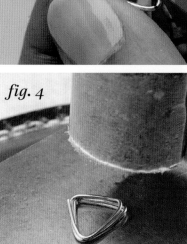

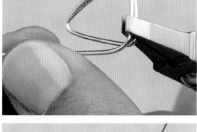

3 Repeat Step 2 two more times, making a total of 3 triangle shapes one on top of the other (**FIG. 3**). Trim the wire in the corner of the triangle so that both cut ends meet exactly.

4 Using the rawhide mallet on the bench block, hammer the triangles to compress the wires. The parallel sides will shift slightly. Hold the piece firmly to maintain its triangular shape while hammering; reshape if needed (**FIG. 4**).

5 Leaving a ½" (1.3 cm) tail, begin wrapping the 22-gauge wire around the triangles. Use chain-nose pliers to pull the wire tightly around the triangle frame, making sure to wrap around and cover the cut ends of the 18-gauge wire (**FIG. 5**). Trim the excess 22-gauge wire on the inside of the link and press down the cut ends with chain-nose pliers to secure.

6 Oxidize the link with liver of sulfur (see page 30) and buff the excess oxidation with steel wool. Tumble to work-harden and polish.

1 Mark the 18-gauge wire ⅝" (1.5 cm) from one end, and again ⅝" (1.5 cm) from the first mark (**FIG. 1**).

2 With flat-nose pliers, bend the wire up 60° at the first mark, pressing firmly against the edge of the pliers. Bend the wire again at the second mark, creating a triangle (**FIG. 2**).

MATERIALS

7¾" (19.5 cm) of 16-gauge pure copper wire

TOOLS

Flat-nose pliers

Round-nose pliers

Flush cutters

Sharpie (or 12 mm mandrel)

Chasing hammer

Rawhide mallet

Steel bench block

Liver of sulfur

Steel wool, #0000

Rotary tumbler with mixed stainless-steel shot

Ruler

FINISHED SIZE

⅞" × 1" (2.2 × 2.5 cm)

LEVEL OF DIFFICULTY

Easy ●○○

WHIRLIGIG

The horseshoe link is reinvented and refined by adding a few simple spirals at each end. Connect the spiral ends of one link to those of another with jump rings to create a stylish wire hinge that can be connected to yet another set of hinged links. Can you visualize a hinged bracelet?

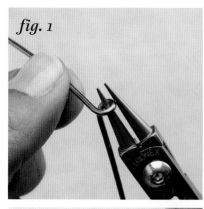

fig. 1

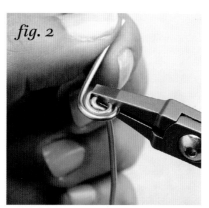

fig. 2

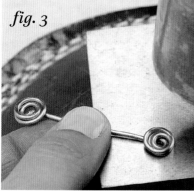

fig. 3

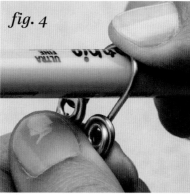

fig. 4

fig. 5

2 After 1½ rotations, hold the spiral with flat-nose pliers and continue spiraling (**FIG. 2**). Coil the wire around and under the previous spiral to create a random look. When only ⅜" (1 cm) of wire remains, tuck the tail wire under the spiral and trim.

3 Repeat Steps 1 and 2 on the other end of the wire.

4 Using your fingers, bend the spirals out so they lie flat. Hammer both sides of each spiral with the rawhide mallet on the bench block to flatten (**FIG. 3**).

5 Center the straight wire on the Sharpie and bend it around to form a horseshoe shape (**FIG. 4**).

6 Using the chasing hammer on the bench block, flatten the curve of the wire slightly (**FIG. 5**).

7 Oxidize the link with liver of sulfur (see page 30) and buff the excess oxidation with steel wool. Tumble to work-harden and polish.

1 Make a 90° bend 3⅛" (7.9 cm) from one end of the wire with flat-nose pliers. Line up the round-nose pliers alongside the longer tail wire and, using the tip of the round-nose pliers, begin making a spiral (see page 27) with the shorter tail wire (**FIG. 1**).

MATERIALS

18" (45.5 cm) of 20-gauge pure copper wire

3" (7.5 cm) of 18-gauge pure copper wire

TOOLS

Chain-nose pliers

Round-nose pliers

Stepped pliers or steel mandrel, 5 mm

Flush cutters

Liver of sulfur

Steel wool, #0000

Rotary tumbler with mixed stainless-steel shot

Ruler

FINISHED SIZE

⅝" × 1" (1.5 × 2.5 cm)

LEVEL OF DIFFICULTY

Moderate ●●○

BALL OF YARN

Make them big or make them small. At any size, wire ball links add interesting dimension to your designs.

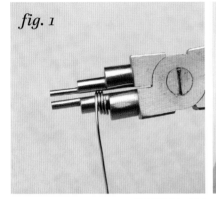

fig. 1

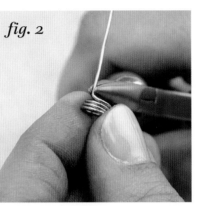

fig. 2

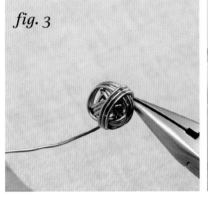

fig. 3

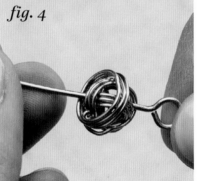

fig. 4

1 To form the base link, coil (see page 24) the 20-gauge wire 3 times around the 5 mm barrel of the stepped pliers (**FIG. 1**). Trim the short tail of the coil.

2 With chain-nose pliers, bend the long tail wire perpendicular to the coil (**FIG. 2**).

3 Hold the coil with chain-nose pliers and wrap the tail loosely around the coil 3 times, keeping the wire rounded as you go to form a ball shape (**FIG. 3**).

4 Repeat Steps 2 and 3 three times, changing directions before wrapping the wire around the coils to form a ball shape.

5 Trim the tail to ⅛" (3 mm) and tuck it into the ball of wire with chain-nose pliers.

6 Make a simple loop (see page 22) on one end of the 18-gauge wire with round-nose pliers. Insert the wire through the center of the ball of wire (**FIG. 4**). Trim the other end of the 18-gauge wire to ⅝" (1.5 cm) and form another simple loop.

7 Oxidize the link with liver of sulfur (see page 30). Buff the excess oxidation with fine steel wool, then tumble to work-harden and polish.

MATERIALS

11" (28 cm) of 16-gauge sterling silver dead-soft wire

TOOLS

Chain-nose pliers

Flat-nose pliers

Round-nose pliers

Flush cutters

Flat hand file

Chasing hammer

Steel bench block

Liver of sulfur

Steel wool, #0000

Rotary tumbler with mixed stainless-steel shot

Ruler

FINISHED SIZE

3⁄8" × 1¼" (1 cm × 3.2 cm)

LEVEL OF DIFFICULTY

Moderate ●●○

TIP

Snug the two coil ends together within the link so they are not loose. To further snug the coils between the simple loops, simply insert the tips of the round-nose pliers and open the coils slightly until you've achieved a tight fit.

BEEHIVE

A pair of wire cages creates a buzz when placed side by side. The finished link is about the size of a bumblebee.

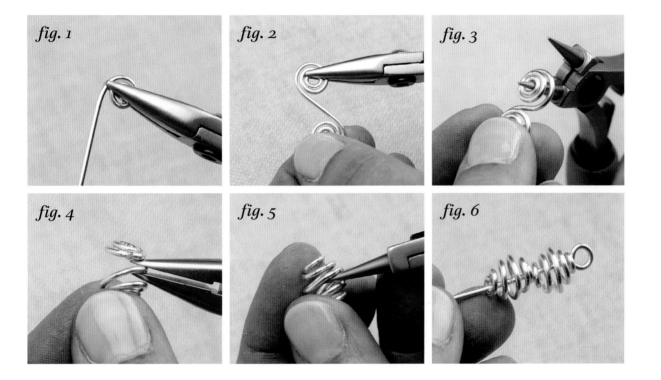

fig. 1

fig. 2

fig. 3

fig. 4

fig. 5

fig. 6

1 Flush-cut two 4¼" (11 cm) pieces of wire. File the ends smooth with a flat hand file. Grasp the tip of the wire with round-nose pliers and form a small loop. Grasp the loop in flat-nose pliers, and begin to make a spiral (see page 27) (**FIG. 1**).

2 On the other end of the wire, begin a second spiral going in the opposite direction. Spiral each end toward the center, alternating each side so that they are equally sized (**FIG. 2**). Stop when both spirals touch.

3 Press the tip of the round-nose pliers through the center of each spiral to space and push out the coils (**FIG. 3**). If necessary, pull the wires up from the top with chain-nose pliers to separate, being careful not to leave marks on the wire.

4 Grasp the center of the link with chain-nose pliers and fold one half over the other (**FIG. 4**).

5 Insert the tips of the round-nose pliers between the loops of the coils to separate them so they are equally spaced (**FIG. 5**). Repeat Steps 1 through 5 with the second

piece of wire. Aim to make both caged beads the same length.

6 Form a simple loop (see page 22) at one end of the remaining 2½" (6.5 cm) piece of wire, using the midpoint on the barrels of the round-nose pliers. Slide both caged beads onto the wire (**FIG. 6**). Trim the cut end of the wire to ⅝" (1.5 cm) and form a second simple loop.

7 Oxidize the link with liver of sulfur (see page 30) and buff the excess oxidation with steel wool. Tumble to polish and soften any tool marks.

TIP

Add extra appeal to this link by using a wire in a contrasting color for the spiral, or add texture to the curves of the "bow" with a chasing hammer!

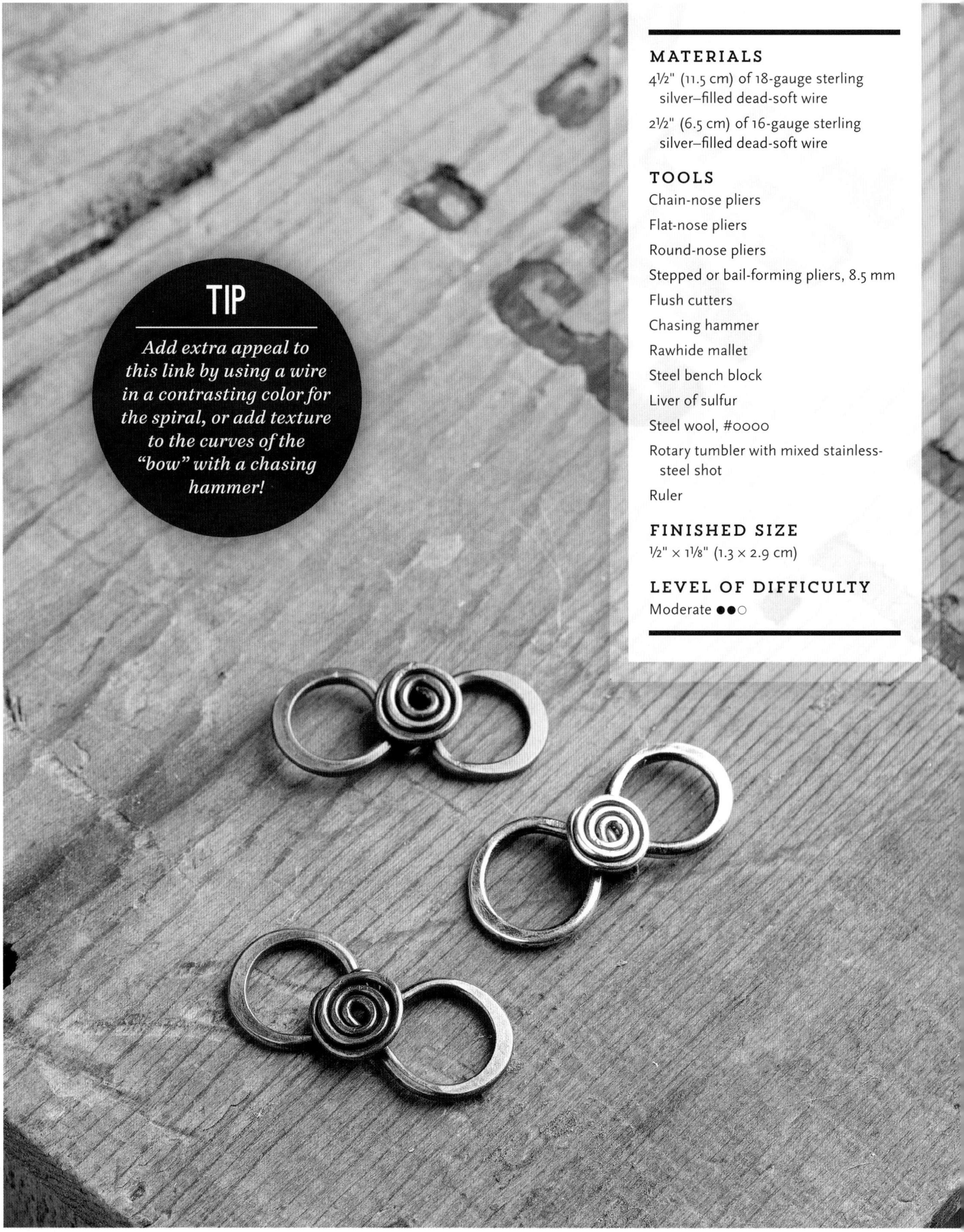

MATERIALS

4½" (11.5 cm) of 18-gauge sterling silver–filled dead-soft wire

2½" (6.5 cm) of 16-gauge sterling silver–filled dead-soft wire

TOOLS

Chain-nose pliers

Flat-nose pliers

Round-nose pliers

Stepped or bail-forming pliers, 8.5 mm

Flush cutters

Chasing hammer

Rawhide mallet

Steel bench block

Liver of sulfur

Steel wool, #0000

Rotary tumbler with mixed stainless-steel shot

Ruler

FINISHED SIZE

½" × 1⅛" (1.3 × 2.9 cm)

LEVEL OF DIFFICULTY

Moderate ●●○

BIRTHDAY BOW

The classic figure-eight link gets a stylish update in this design. Adding a wire spiral gives the link a lively look.

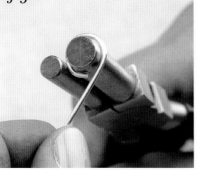

fig. 1

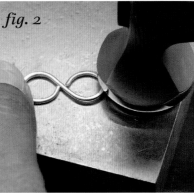

fig. 2

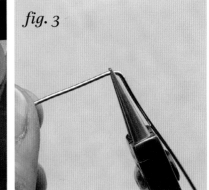

fig. 3

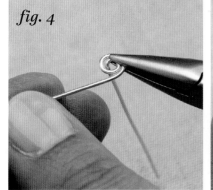

fig. 4

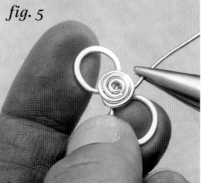

fig. 5

the round-nose pliers and make a small loop, which will be the beginning of a spiral (see page 27) (**FIG. 4**).

7 Grasp the loop with chain-nose pliers and continue making the spiral until 3⁄8" (1 cm) of horizontal wire remains. Bend the tail under the spiral with chain-nose pliers and trim.

8 Place the spiral on the center of the figure-eight link. Wrap the tail wire around the middle of the link, passing once on each side of the spiral. Pull the wire tightly with chain-nose pliers as you wrap (**FIG. 5**). Trim the wire on the underside of the link.

9 Hammer the spiral with the chasing hammer on the bench block to flatten slightly and secure.

10 Oxidize the link with liver of sulfur (see page 30) and buff the excess oxidation with steel wool. Tumble to work-harden and polish.

1 Grasp the end of the 16-gauge wire with the 8.5 mm barrel of the bail-forming pliers and form a simple loop (see page 22) (**FIG. 1**).

2 Repeat Step 1 with the other end of the wire, making a loop in the opposite direction, forming a figure eight.

3 Work-harden the link by hammering gently with the rawhide mallet on the bench block, concentrating on the center.

4 Flatten each side of the curve slightly with the chasing hammer on the bench block (**FIG. 2**). Close any gaps in the circle with flat-nose pliers.

5 Make a 90° bend in the 18-gauge wire with chain-nose pliers 2¼" (5.5 cm) from one end of the wire (**FIG. 3**).

6 Hold the wire upright, with one tail pointing down. Hold the round-nose pliers parallel to the vertical wire. Grasp the corner of the horizontal wire with the tip of

TIP

Hold the coil in place firmly as you form the first wrapped loop. It will tend to slide down, and you want to be sure the wraps are trapping the coiled wire.

COILED HORSESHOE

By wrapping a few coils over the top of the Coiled Horseshoe, the traditional link gets a modern design boost.

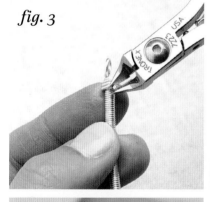

fig. 1

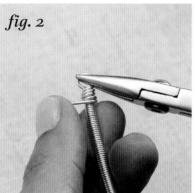

fig. 2

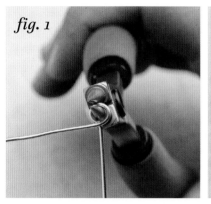

fig. 3

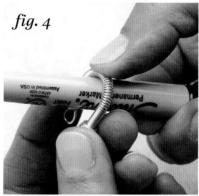

fig. 4

fig. 5

1 Using the coiling tool, form a coil (see page 24) with the entire length of 22-gauge silver wire. Slide the coil off the tool and trim to 1½" (3.8 cm). Set the coil aside.

2 Mark the 18-gauge wire 3¼" (8.5 cm) from one end with the Sharpie. Using the middle of the round-nose pliers, form the first half of a wrapped loop (see page 23) at the mark in the wire (**FIG. 1**).

3 Slide the coil onto the long part of the wire. Complete the wrapped loop, holding the loop with chain-nose pliers and wrapping the tail wire over the end of the coil 5 times (**FIG. 2**).

4 Make a second wrapped loop at the other end of the wire, repeating Step 3, and trim the excess wire (**FIG. 3**).

5 Place the middle of the coil on the thickest portion of the Sharpie and bend it down carefully to form a U-shape (**FIG. 4**).

6 Grasp one loop with flat-nose pliers and bend it back slightly to straighten. Repeat on the other loop. The loops should be parallel to each other (**FIG. 5**).

7 Oxidize the link with liver of sulfur (see page 30) and buff the excess oxidation with steel wool. Tumble to work-harden and polish.

MATERIALS

20" (51 cm) of 22-gauge pure copper wire

6½" (16.5 cm) of 18-gauge sterling silver dead-soft wire

TOOLS

Chain-nose pliers

Flat-nose pliers

Round-nose pliers

Coiling tool or steel mandrel, 2 mm

Flush cutters

Rawhide mallet

Steel bench block

Sharpie (or 12 mm mandrel)

Liver of sulfur

Steel wool, #0000

Rotary tumbler with mixed stainless-steel shot

Ruler

FINISHED SIZE

¾" × 1¼" (2 × 3.2 cm)

LEVEL OF DIFFICULTY

Moderate ●●○

TIPS

Be sure to either hammer the loops with a rawhide mallet or tumble to work-harden the links, as this design features open loops, and work-hardening will ensure they do not open further.

Building a chain with this link is easy; simply open the loop and attach to another link!

CORONA

Combine both smooth and coiled wire to create
a striking link in any color combination!

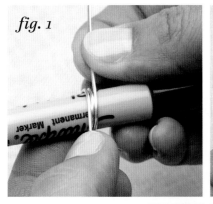

fig. 1

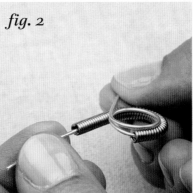

fig. 2

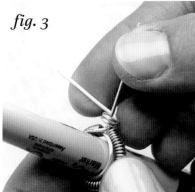

fig. 3

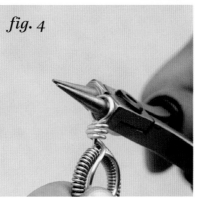

fig. 4

4 Reinsert the loops onto the Sharpie to help maintain the circular shape. With chain-nose pliers, bend the shorter wire straight up, perpendicular to the loops. Bring the longer wire around the right of the short tail and wrap it around 3 times; trim on the back of the link (**FIG. 3**) and pinch in the end with chain-nose pliers.

5 Trim the short wire to ¾" (2 cm) and bend it forward to a 90° angle. Using the back of the round-nose pliers, roll the wire forward to form a simple loop (see page 22) (**FIG. 4**). Work-harden the simple loop with the rawhide mallet on the bench block.

6 Oxidize the link in liver of sulfur (see page 30). (Sterling silver and copper wire oxidize at different rates; therefore, you may need to leave the links in the solution longer or redip the link a second time in fresh liver of sulfur solution.) Buff the excess oxidation with steel wool. Tumble to work-harden and polish.

1 Using the coiling tool, coil (see page 24) the entire length of the 22-gauge copper wire. Slide the coil off the tool and trim to 1½" (3.8 cm); set aside.

2 Make a mark with the Sharpie 4¾" (12 cm) at one end of the 18-gauge sterling silver wire. Place the widest point of the Sharpie perpendicular to the wire at the mark. Hold the wire in place with your thumb and wrap the longer piece of wire down and around the Sharpie twice, stopping when the tail wires cross (**FIG. 1**). Remove the wire loop from the Sharpie.

3 With the loops facing you, as shown, slide the coil onto the left-hand tail wire and feed the coil around the bottom loop to make a complete circle (**FIG. 2**). The top loop will be plain.

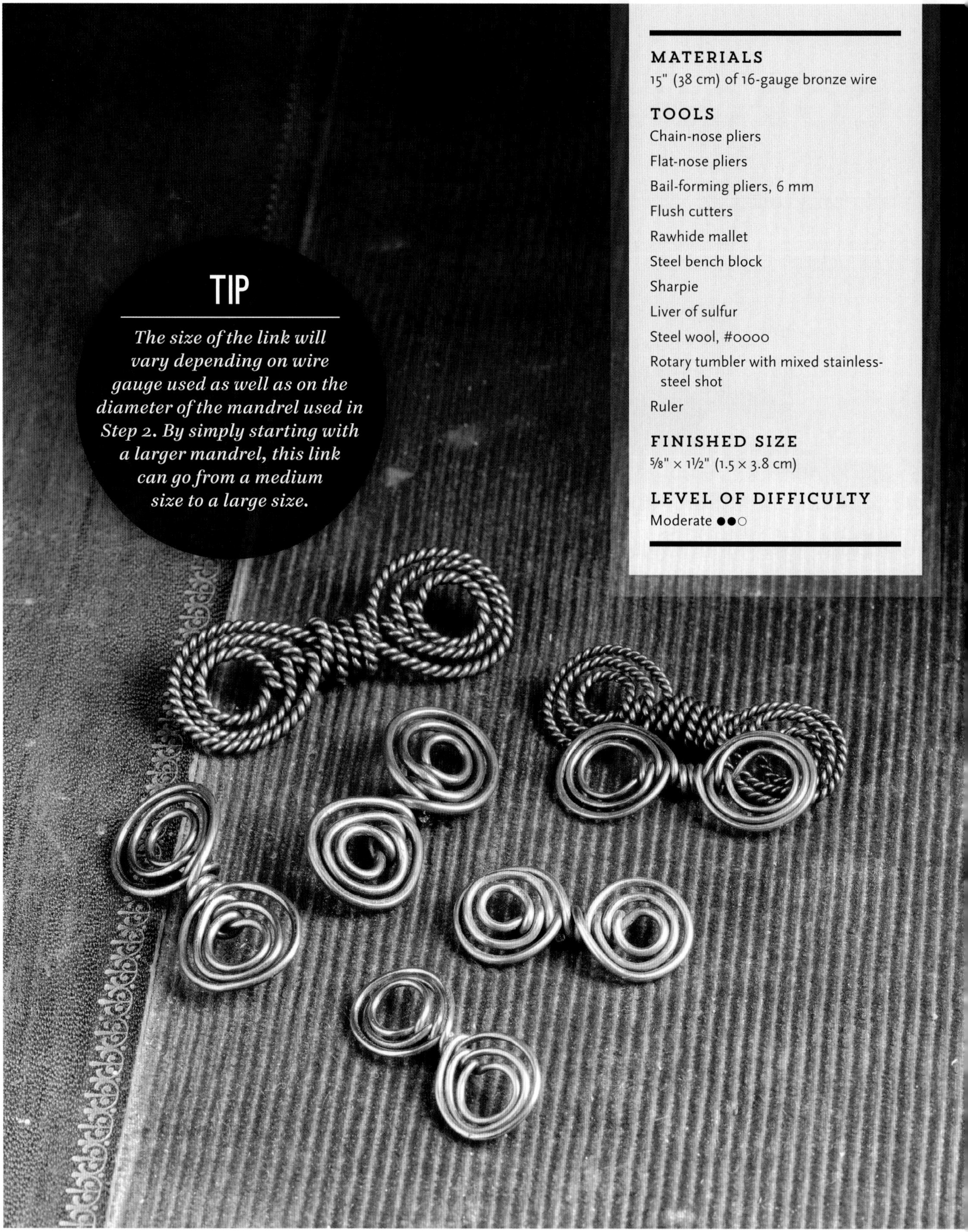

TIP

The size of the link will vary depending on wire gauge used as well as on the diameter of the mandrel used in Step 2. By simply starting with a larger mandrel, this link can go from a medium size to a large size.

MATERIALS

15" (38 cm) of 16-gauge bronze wire

TOOLS

- Chain-nose pliers
- Flat-nose pliers
- Bail-forming pliers, 6 mm
- Flush cutters
- Rawhide mallet
- Steel bench block
- Sharpie
- Liver of sulfur
- Steel wool, #0000
- Rotary tumbler with mixed stainless-steel shot
- Ruler

FINISHED SIZE

$\frac{5}{8}$" × 1$\frac{1}{2}$" (1.5 × 3.8 cm)

LEVEL OF DIFFICULTY

Moderate ●●○

OWL EYES

With its flowing curves, the Owl Eyes link can double as a connector or an attractive focal point—just vary the gauge of wire and mandrel diameter!

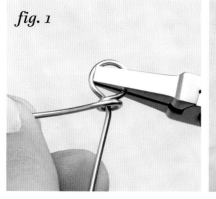
fig. 1

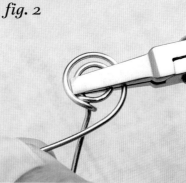
fig. 2

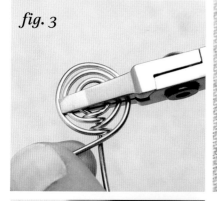
fig. 3

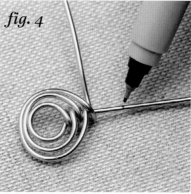
fig. 4

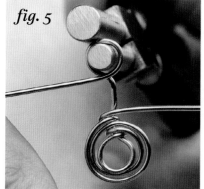
fig. 5

3 Hold the loop with flat-nose pliers. Using your fingers, carefully shape the tail wire around the first loop to create a second loop, keeping the wire rounded as you go (**FIG. 2**). Wrap the tail wire once around the core wire. Repeat to create a third loop, wrapping the tail wire once around the core wire (**FIG. 3**).

4 Measure from the start of the wrap on the inside loop to the bottom of the last wrap on the outside loop. Mark that length on the core wire with a Sharpie (**FIG. 4**).

5 Begin a wrapped loop at the mark using the 6 mm barrel of the bail-forming pliers, then wrap this tail wire once around the core wire (**FIG. 5**). Repeat Step 3. Fill in any bare space around the core wire by wrapping it with the tail wire. Trim the tail wires on the back side of the link and press the cut ends down with chain-nose pliers.

6 Hammer the loop section with the rawhide mallet on the bench block to flatten if necessary.

7 Oxidize the link with liver of sulfur (see page 30) and buff the excess oxidation with steel wool. Tumble to work-harden and polish.

1 Mark the middle of the wire with a Sharpie.

2 Begin a wrapped loop (see page 23) at the mark using the 6 mm barrel of the bail-forming pliers, then wrap the tail wire once around the core wire (**FIG. 1**).

MATERIALS

6" (15 cm) of 16-gauge pure copper
square wire

3" (7.5 cm) of 14-gauge sterling silver
dead-soft wire

TOOLS

Chain-nose pliers

Flat-nose pliers

Round-nose pliers

Flush cutters

Flat hand file

Chasing hammer

Rawhide mallet

Steel bench block

Sharpie (or 12 mm mandrel)

Liver of sulfur

Steel wool, #0000

Rotary tumbler with mixed stainless-
steel shot

Ruler

FINISHED SIZE

⅝" × 1⅛" (1.5 cm × 2.9 cm)

LEVEL OF DIFFICULTY

Moderate ●●○

TIPS

Create endless variations for this link: copper wire on copper, brass with sterling, round wire instead of square wire.

Copper wire usually oxidizes faster than sterling silver when placed together in the same solution. Leave the silver link in longer to darken sufficiently. You can run the link under hot water before adding it to the oxidizing solution.

SNOCONE

Mix two wirework favorites—the simple loop
and a spiral—and you'll have one playful link!

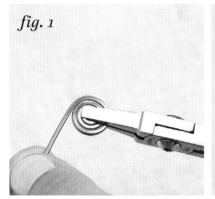

fig. 1

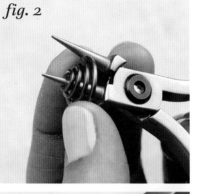

fig. 2

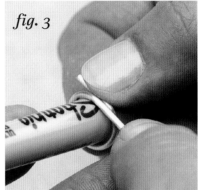

fig. 3

fig. 4

fig. 5

1 Use the file to smooth the ends of the 16-gauge wire. At one end, make a small loop with round-nose pliers. Grasp the loop with flat-nose pliers and make a spiral (see page 27) by hand-winding the rest of the wire around the loop (**FIG. 1**). Flush-cut the wire end.

2 Place the spiral on the bench block and hammer lightly with the chasing hammer.

3 Push the center of the spiral up with the tip of the round-nose pliers and stretch out the coil, spacing the coils evenly (**FIG. 2**). Set the coil aside.

4 Hold one end of the 14-gauge wire with your thumb against the thickest part of the Sharpie and wrap the wire around it 1¼ times (**FIG. 3**).

5 Keep the loop on the Sharpie to maintain its round shape. Where the wires begin to touch, bend

the longer wire up perpendicular to the loop with chain-nose pliers (**FIG. 4**). Trim the shorter wire flush at the bend, creating a complete circle.

6 Flatten the curve of the loop with the chasing hammer on the bench block, then hammer the loop with the rounded end of the hammer to texture.

7 Insert the tail of the 14-gauge wire into the center of the domed coil, then trim the tail to ⅝" (1.5 cm), and file the end. Bend the wire forward 90° with chain-nose pliers. Grasp the end of the wire with the back of the round-nose pliers and roll forward, forming a simple loop (see page 22) (**FIG. 5**).

8 Oxidize the link in a hot solution of liver of sulfur (see page 30) and buff the excess oxidation with steel wool. Tumble to work-harden and polish.

TIPS

As you form this link, keep the wires as parallel as possible to preserve a nice rectangular shape.

Press the wires firmly against the edge of the flat-nose pliers to achieve a sharp-looking bend.

Create a horizontal rectangle link instead of a vertical rectangle! Merely form the simple loop on the long edge of the link rather than at the short end.

SPRINGBOARD

A simple coil takes a geometric twist in this link. Go from a vertical to horizontal rectangle with the placement of the loop.

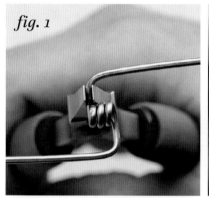

fig. 1

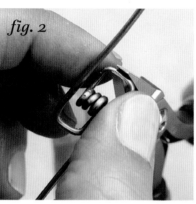

fig. 2

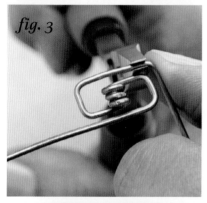

fig. 3

fig. 4

fig. 5

3 Grasp one wire next to the bend with flat-nose pliers and make another bend downward against the edge of the pliers, forming another right angle. Repeat on the opposite tail wire (**FIG. 2**).

4 Holding the link with the tail wires running horizontally, insert the flat-nose pliers as shown and bend the wire downward, pressing against the edge of the flat-nose pliers (**FIG. 3**). Repeat on the opposite tail wire. Hammer with the rawhide mallet on the bench block to flatten the link if necessary.

5 Measure and mark one tail wire ¾" (2 cm) from the middle of the short end of the link (**FIG. 4**). Flush-cut the wire at the mark and file with a few passes of the flat file.

6 Form a simple loop (see page 22) using the back of the round-nose pliers (**FIG. 5**). Repeat Steps 5 and 6 with the opposite tail wire.

7 Hammer the ends of the link with the rawhide mallet on the bench block to work-harden.

8 Oxidize the link with liver of sulfur (see page 30) and buff the excess oxidation with the steel wool. Tumble to work-harden and polish.

1 Grasp the center of the wire with the 2 mm barrel of the stepped pliers and coil (see page 24) 3 times. The tail wires will point in opposite directions.

2 Using flat-nose pliers, grasp one tail wire just above the coil. Bend the wire over the edge of the pliers into a right angle. Repeat on the opposite tail wire, with the wires pointing in opposite directions (**FIG. 1**).

MATERIALS

7" (18 cm) of 26-gauge sterling silver half-hard wire

Spool of 12-gauge pure copper wire

TOOLS

Chain-nose pliers

Flat-nose pliers

Stepped pliers or steel mandrel, 7 mm

Flush cutters, heavy-duty

Flat hand file

Chasing hammer

Steel bench block

Two-hole screw-down punch (1.6 mm)

Sharpie

Liver of sulfur

Steel wool, #0000

Rotary tumbler with mixed stainless-steel shot

Ruler

FINISHED SIZE

½" × 1⅛" (1.3 × 2.9 cm)

LEVEL OF DIFFICULTY

Moderate ●●○

TIP

Have fun adding a variety of textures to the figure eight with design stamps and texturizing hammers.

STITCHED FIGURE EIGHT

Heavy-gauge wire is the foundation for this hammered and textured wire link. Stitched wire in a contrasting metal adds an artful design embellishment.

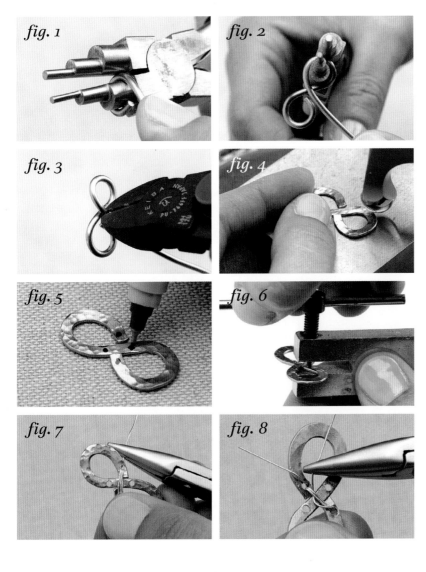

fig. 1

fig. 2

fig. 3

fig. 4

fig. 5

fig. 6

fig. 7

fig. 8

3 Flatten the wire with the chasing hammer on the bench block, then texture the wire with the rounded end of the hammer (**FIG. 4**). Use flat-nose pliers to close any gap in the wire caused by hammering.

4 Measure ⅛" (3 mm) from the center of the figure eight and mark with a Sharpie. Mark 3 more equidistant dots on the inside of the figure eight (**FIG. 5**).

5 Using the 1.6 mm punch on the two-hole punch, screw down the handle at the first mark to make a hole (**FIG. 6**). Repeat, punching the remaining 3 holes.

6 Cut 3½" (9 cm) of 26-gauge wire. Leaving a 1" (2.5 cm) tail, stitch the wire diagonally through 2 holes. Pull the wire through the holes a total of 3 times, tightening the wire by pulling with chain-nose pliers (**FIG. 7**). Tuck the wire tails under the wraps, then trim any excess wire (**FIG. 8**). Press the wire down gently with flat-nose pliers to secure the stitches.

7 Repeat Step 6, stitching the remaining diagonal holes and crossing over the first set of stitches. Once completed, hammer the wires 2 or 3 times on the bench block to flatten slightly and secure the stitching.

8 Oxidize the link with liver of sulfur (see page 30) and buff the excess oxidation with steel wool. Tumble to work-harden and polish.

1 Working from the spool of 12-gauge wire, flush-cut the end of the wire with heavy-duty cutters and file smooth. Using the 7 mm barrel of the stepped pliers, rotate the wire away from you to form a simple loop (**FIG. 1**). Remove the pliers.

2 Place the 7 mm barrel of the stepped pliers above the loop and wrap the wire around the barrel until it intersects with the first loop, forming a figure eight (**FIG. 2**). Flush-cut the wire, making sure you have a complete loop (**FIG. 3**). File the end of the wire smooth.

TIPS

Reinsert the bail-forming pliers into the loops to ensure they are a nice round shape.

For a design variation, fan out the loops by holding the top and bottom loops with flat-nose pliers and pulling them out. The link will resemble miniature wings.

TRIPLE LOOP

With less than a foot of wire, you can make this seemingly complex-looking link as easy as one, two, three!

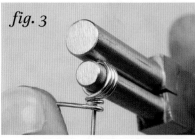
fig. 1

fig. 2

fig. 3

fig. 4

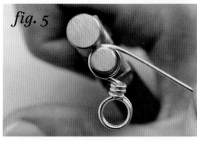
fig. 5

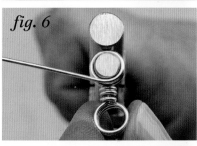
fig. 6

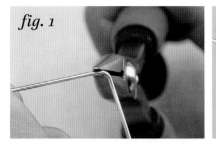
fig. 7

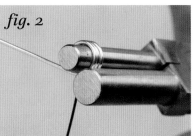
fig. 8

1 Mark the wire 4½" (11.5 cm) from one end and make a 90° bend at the mark with chain-nose pliers (**FIG. 1**).

2 Grasp the wire at the bend with the bail-forming pliers and wrap the wire 3 times around the 6 mm barrel. The wire tails should form a 90° angle (**FIG. 2**).

3 Keeping the loops on the pliers, wrap the tail wire around the longer wire for 3 wraps, then trim the tail. (**FIG. 3**).

4 Bend the long wire up 90° (**FIG. 4**). Remove the pliers.

5 Turn the loop upside down and place the bail-forming pliers at the bend. Wrap the long wire 3 times around the 6 mm barrel (**FIG. 5**). Reposition the loops by pushing them up slightly so that they are lined up with the first set of loops (**FIG. 6**).

6 Hold the loops to maintain the shape and wrap the tail wire around the previous wraps at the center of the link. Keep the wires parallel as you wrap (**FIG. 7**). Trim the tail wire and tuck in the end with chain-nose pliers.

7 Insert the tip of the round-nose pliers between the end loops to spread them apart slightly (**FIG. 8**).

8 Oxidize the link with liver of sulfur (see page 30) and buff the excess oxidation with steel wool. Tumble to work-harden and polish.

MATERIALS

Spool of 12-gauge pure copper wire, 1⅜" (3.5 cm) used

15" (38 cm) of 20-gauge pure copper wire

TOOLS

Chain-nose pliers, 2 pairs

Flat-nose pliers

Round-nose pliers

Stepped pliers or steel mandrel, 8 mm

Flush cutters, heavy-duty

Chasing hammer

Rawhide mallet

Steel bench block

Liver of sulfur

Steel wool, #0000

Rotary tumbler with mixed stainless-steel shot

Ruler

FINISHED SIZE

1" (2.5 cm) diameter

LEVEL OF DIFFICULTY

More challenging ●●●

TIPS

Use heavy-duty flush cutters to cut the 12-gauge wire for the jump rings so you won't damage the blades of your regular wire cutters.

The sky's the limit when it comes to adding texture and detail to the jump ring! Before making the wire petals, use texturizing hammers or decorative stamps on the jump ring to add variety to each Blossom link.

The 20-gauge wire stiffens as you work with it. To make the petals easier to manipulate, substitute 22-gauge wire.

BLOSSOM

The base of this sweet flower link looks like a washer—but it is really just flattened heavy-gauge wire.

fig. 1

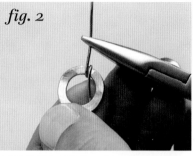
fig. 2

fig. 3

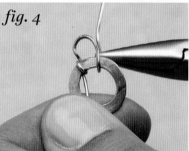
fig. 4

fig. 5

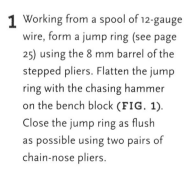
fig. 6

edge of the jump ring. Wrap the 20-gauge wire up and around the back of the bottom jaw to create a petal shape (**FIG. 3**).

4 Hold the petal with your fingers to maintain its shape and pull the tail wire through the jump ring, from front to back. Pull the wire around the jump ring tightly, using chain-nose pliers (**FIG. 4**). Keep the wire rounded and loose so as not to create kinks. Reinsert the round-nose pliers into the petal to reshape if necessary.

5 Press the wrapped wires down against the jump ring with chain-nose pliers.

6 Repeat Steps 3 through 5 to create a total of 7 or 8 petals (**FIG. 5**). Trim the tail wires at the inside edge of the jump ring; press down with chain-nose pliers to secure.

7 Reinsert the back of the bottom jaw of the round-nose pliers into each of the petals to round and reshape if necessary.

8 Hammer the center of the flower and edges of the petals lightly with the chasing hammer on the bench block (**FIG. 6**).

9 Oxidize the link with liver of sulfur (see page 30) and buff the excess oxidation with steel wool. Tumble to work-harden and polish.

1 Working from a spool of 12-gauge wire, form a jump ring (see page 25) using the 8 mm barrel of the stepped pliers. Flatten the jump ring with the chasing hammer on the bench block (**FIG. 1**). Close the jump ring as flush as possible using two pairs of chain-nose pliers.

2 Leaving a 1" (2.5 cm) tail, wrap the 20-gauge wire once around the jump ring, covering the cut ends of the jump ring and ending on the back of the washer. Pull the wire tightly with chain-nose pliers (**FIG. 2**).

3 Place the back of the bottom jaw of the round-nose pliers on the

MATERIALS

16" (40.5 cm) of 18-gauge brass wire

TOOLS

Chain-nose pliers

Flat-nose pliers

Round-nose pliers

Flush cutters

Oxidizing agent (Novacan Black, JAX)

Steel wool, #0000

Rotary tumbler with mixed stainless-
steel shot

FINISHED SIZE

Varies

LEVEL OF DIFFICULTY

More challenging ●●●

CUMULUS CLOUDS

Add a touch of whimsy with this swirly link. Vary the placement
and size of the open spirals so that no two links are exactly alike.

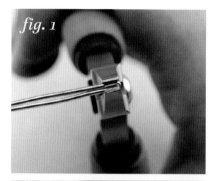
fig. 1

fig. 2

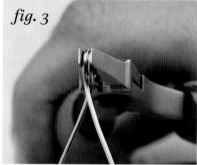
fig. 3

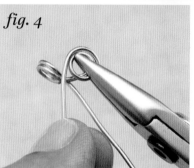
fig. 4

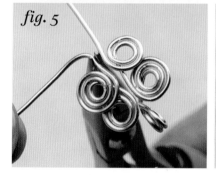
fig. 5

fig. 6

4 Grasp one of the tail wires close to the loop with round-nose pliers. Wrap the wire around one barrel to create a loop. Grasp the loop with chain-nose pliers and form a spiral (see page 27) around the loop, making at least one additional turn (**FIG. 4**).

5 Repeat Step 4 with the other tail wire, varying the placement of the loop and number of spirals (**FIG. 5**). Repeat Step 4 again with each wire, creating a total of 4 spirals in varying sizes. End with both tail wires vertical and parallel to each other, opposite the loop on the other end.

6 Using chain-nose pliers, bend one tail wire at a 90° angle. Wrap this wire once around the other tail wire and trim; tuck in the end with chain-nose pliers.

7 Form a wrapped loop with the remaining tail wire, making the loop the same size as the first loop and wrapping over the previous wrap (**FIG. 6**). Trim the wire and tuck in the end with chain-nose pliers.

8 Oxidize the link with the oxidizing agent for brass (see page 30) and buff the excess oxidation with steel wool. Tumble to work-harden and polish.

1 Bend the wire in half and squeeze the bend tightly with flat-nose pliers (**FIG. 1**). Straighten the wires so they are parallel.

2 Grasp the wires at the bend with round-nose pliers and form

a simple loop (see page 22) (**FIG. 2**). Center the loop over the wires using chain-nose pliers.

3 Hold the loop with flat-nose pliers and cross the wires slightly (**FIG. 3**).

MATERIALS
14" (35.5 cm) of 18-gauge pure
copper wire

TOOLS
Flat-nose pliers

Round-nose pliers

Bail-forming pliers or steel mandrel,
6 mm

Flush cutters

Rawhide mallet

Steel bench block

Sharpie

Liver of sulfur

Steel wool, #0000

Rotary tumbler with mixed stainless-
steel shot

Ruler

FINISHED SIZE
⅞" × 1¼" (2.2 × 3.2 cm)

LEVEL OF DIFFICULTY
More challenging ●●●

TIPS

*Once the link is completed,
use flat-nose pliers to readjust
the spacing between coils so that
it is even throughout.*

*An hour in the tumbler will
help to maintain the entire
shape of this coiled link.*

CURLICUE

Move beyond traditional link styles and create some playful volume with this Slinky-style link.

fig. 1

fig. 2

fig. 3

fig. 4

fig. 5

fig. 6

1 Mark the wire 1½" (3.8 cm) from one end with the Sharpie. Grasp the wire at the mark with the 6 mm barrel of the bail-forming pliers and coil (see page 24) the wire around the barrel for 12 complete turns. The tail wires should be directly across from each other on either end of the coil (**FIG. 1**).

2 Grasp one end of the coil with flat-nose pliers and gently stretch out the coil (**FIG. 2**).

3 Using your fingers, pull the ends of the coil around to form a circle (**FIG. 3**).

4 Cross the tail wires, forming an X (**FIG. 4**).

5 Use chain-nose pliers to bend the tail wires slightly so the wires form a right angle to each other (**FIG. 5**). Wrap the horizontal wire around the vertical wire twice and trim.

6 Bend the vertical wire at a 90° angle to the side of the link. Trim the wire to ¾" (2 cm). Grasp the wire with the back of the round-nose pliers and form a simple loop (see page 22) (**FIG. 6**). Work-harden the loop with the rawhide mallet on the bench block.

7 Oxidize the link with liver of sulfur (see page 30) and buff with steel wool. Tumble to work-harden and polish.

MATERIALS

5½" (14 cm) of 18-gauge sterling silver dead-soft wire

TOOLS

Chain-nose pliers

Flat-nose pliers

Bail-forming pliers or steel mandrel, 6 mm and 8.5 mm

Flush cutters

Rawhide mallet

Steel bench block

Liver of sulfur

Steel wool, #0000

Rotary tumbler with mixed stainless-steel shot

FINISHED SIZE

½" × ⅞" (1.3 × 2.2 cm)

LEVEL OF DIFFICULTY

More challenging ●●●

TIP

A thinner gauge of wire was used to create this link so that the wire would be somewhat flexible. To help the link maintain its shape once it is completed, leave it in the tumbler for 1 hour to work-harden thoroughly.

DOUBLE INFINITY

With just a few turns of the pliers, create this deceptively
simple infinity-style link.

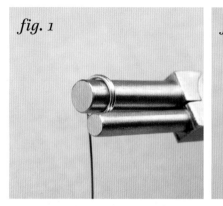

fig. 1

fig. 2

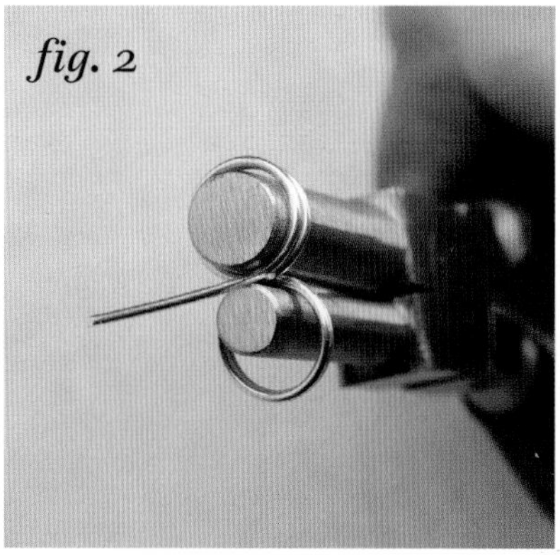

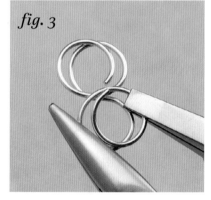

fig. 3

3 With the cut ends facing up, grasp the upper bottom loop with flat-nose pliers and grasp the lower bottom loop with chain-nose pliers. Holding the flat-nose pliers on the right side steady, gently pull the chain-nose pliers to the left slightly, pulling the side of the loop without the cut end so that the shape will not be distorted (**FIG. 3**).

4 Turn the link over and repeat Step 3 with the other double loop, pulling the loop to the left so that the space created in the center matches that of the first double loop. The cut ends of the wire should rest on the inside rim of the loops.

5 With the rawhide mallet and bench block, hammer each side of the link slightly to work-harden (**FIG. 4**). Tweak as needed.

6 Oxidize the link with liver of sulfur (see page 30) and buff with steel wool. Tumble to work-harden and polish.

1 Grasp the tip of one end of the wire with the 8.5 mm barrel of the bail-forming pliers. Rotate the pliers to form a double loop (**FIG. 1**), coiling the wire twice around that barrel. Remove the pliers.

2 Insert the 6 mm barrel of the bail-forming pliers into the double loop, with the 8.5 mm barrel on top of the cut end of the double loop. Wrap the tail wire up and around the 8.5 mm barrel; remove the pliers. Reinsert the 8.5 mm barrel into the new loop just made, completing 2 full rotations (**FIG. 2**). Trim the tail wire where it meets the end of the first double loop, with the cut sides of the loops on the same side of the link.

MATERIALS

12" (30.5 cm) of 22-gauge sterling silver half-round, half-hard wire

26" (66 cm) of 22-gauge sterling silver half-hard wire

Spool of 16-gauge sterling silver dead-soft wire, 6½" (16.5 cm) used

TOOLS

Chain-nose pliers

Flat-nose pliers

Round-nose pliers

Stepped pliers or steel mandrel, 5 mm

Coiling tool or steel mandrel, 2 mm

Flush cutters

Rawhide mallet

Steel bench block

Sharpie

Liver of sulfur

Steel wool, #0000

Rotary tumbler with mixed stainless-steel shot

Ruler

FINISHED SIZE

⅝" × 1⅜" (1.5 × 3.5 cm)

LEVEL OF DIFFICULTY

More challenging ●●●

ELLIPTICAL ILLUSION

Featuring graceful curves and a rich patina, this elliptical link
is created with three types of wire for added contrast.

fig. 1

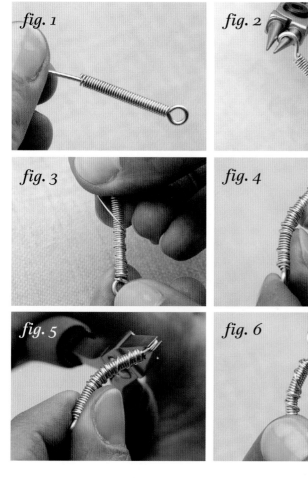

fig. 3

fig. 5

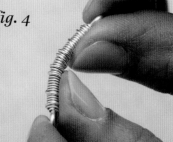

fig. 2

fig. 4

fig. 6

1 Working from a spool of 16-gauge wire, flush-cut the end of the wire. Grasp the tip of the wire with the 5 mm barrel of the stepped pliers and coil (see page 24) the wire around that barrel twice; remove the coil. Flush-cut the coil into 2 jump rings (see page 25). With the rawhide mallet and bench block, hammer each ring several times to work-harden. Set aside.

2 Using the coiling tool, form a coil with the 26" (66 cm) length of 22-gauge half-hard wire. Cut the coil in half to create two 1" (2.5 cm) coils and set aside.

3 Flush-cut two 2¼" (5.5 cm) lengths of 16-gauge wire.

4 Make a simple loop (see page 22) on the end of one 16-gauge wire

with the middle of the round-nose pliers. Slide a coil onto the wire (**FIG. 1**).

5 Trim the remaining tail to ½" (1.3 cm). Bend the wire back 90° with chain-nose pliers to form a second simple loop, with the cut ends of the loops on the same side of the link (**FIG. 2**).

6 Cut 6" (15 cm) of 22-gauge half-round wire. Wrap the wire randomly around the coiled wire, pulling tightly (**FIG. 3**). Trim the ends. Press the ends in with chain-nose pliers to secure.

7 With your thumbs, bend the coil into a rounded oval shape (**FIG. 4**). Repeat Steps 4 through 7 with the second wire.

8 Grasp the simple loop with flat-nose pliers and bend it back slightly (**FIG. 5**). Repeat for all 4 simple loops. Place the 2 coils together to form an oval; the loops should be parallel to one another.

9 Open a jump ring from Step 1 and attach it to the simple loops on one end of the 2 coils (**FIG. 6**). Repeat, attaching a jump ring to the loops on the other end of the coils.

10 Oxidize the link with liver of sulfur (see page 30) and buff the excess oxidation with steel wool. Tumble to work-harden and polish.

TIP

Squeeze the flat-nose pliers several times up the length of the folded wires to ensure the wires are completely straight.

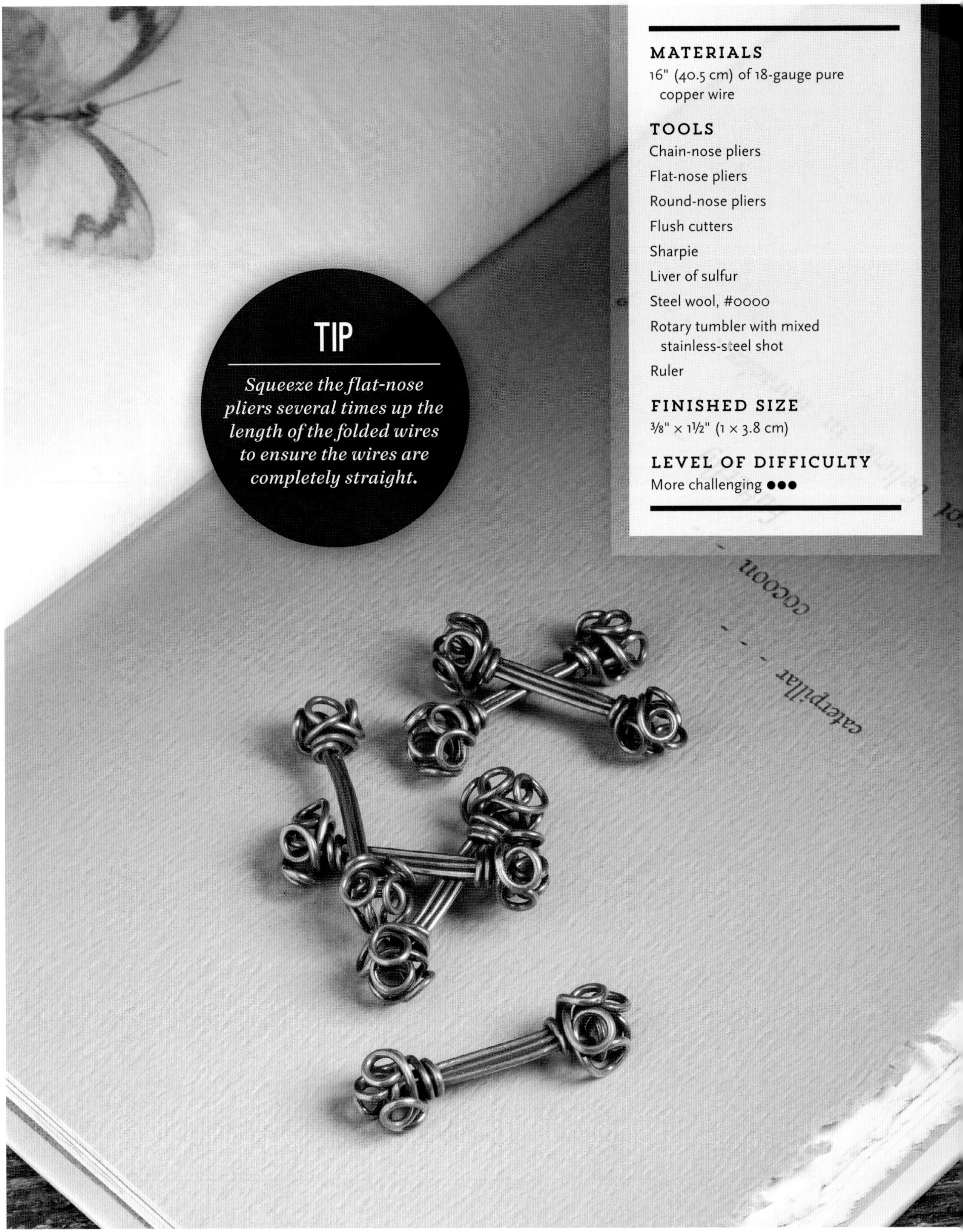

MATERIALS

16" (40.5 cm) of 18-gauge pure copper wire

TOOLS

Chain-nose pliers

Flat-nose pliers

Round-nose pliers

Flush cutters

Sharpie

Liver of sulfur

Steel wool, #0000

Rotary tumbler with mixed stainless-steel shot

Ruler

FINISHED SIZE

3/8" × 1½" (1 × 3.8 cm)

LEVEL OF DIFFICULTY

More challenging ●●●

MAJORETTES

Set your jewelry apart with this long wireworked link. The open balled ends, formed by a cluster of loops, provide an easy way to make attachments.

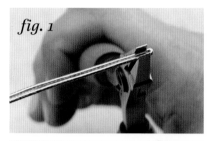
fig. 1

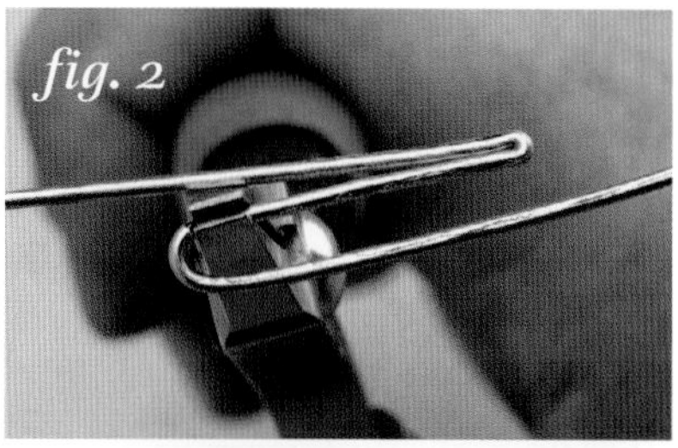

fig. 2

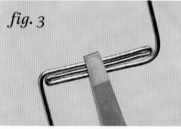
fig. 3

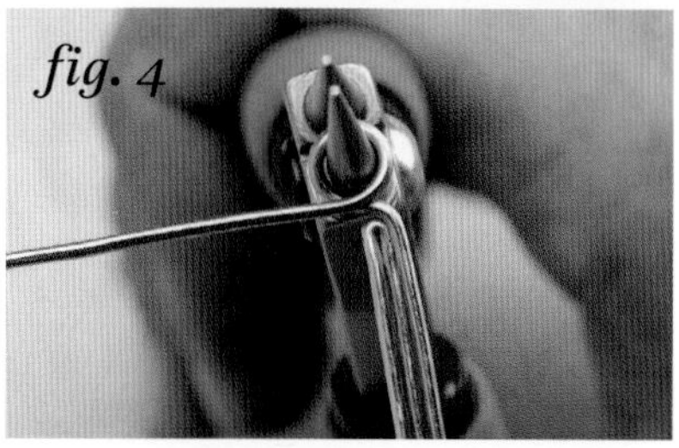

fig. 4

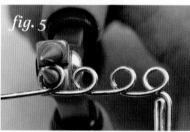
fig. 5

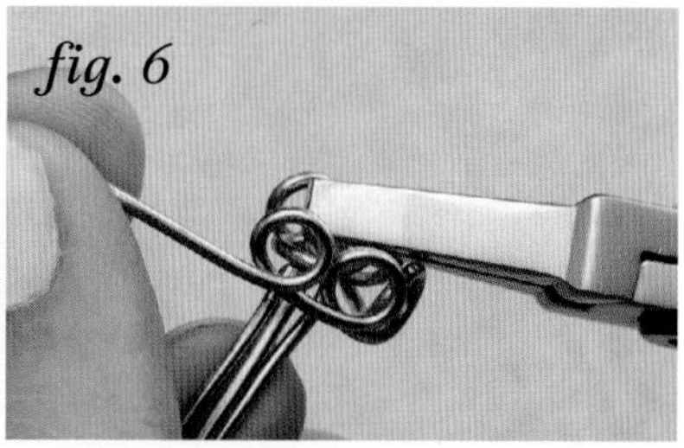

fig. 6

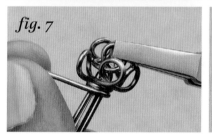
fig. 7

fig. 8

horizontal. Bend the left tail wire down 90° around the fold, then flip the wire and repeat with the other tail wire. The wires will point in opposite directions (**FIG. 3**).

4   Take the tail wire on one end of the link and, working three-quarters of the way toward the back of the jaws of the round-nose pliers, make the first part of a wrapped loop (see page 23) just above the folded end (**FIG. 4**).

5   Measure ¼" (6 mm) from the first loop and make a second loop. Repeat for a total of 6 loops (**FIG. 5**).

6   Hold the first loop with flat-nose pliers, then bend the looped wire down and around the first loop, encircling it (**FIG. 6**).

7   Wrap the tail wire around the stem of the folded wires twice (**FIG. 7**); trim. Press the cut end down with chain-nose pliers to secure. Repeat Steps 4 through 7 with the other tail wire.

8   Using chain-nose pliers, press the loops inward slightly and reshape as needed to create a rounded ball shape (**FIG. 8**).

9   Oxidize the link with liver of sulfur (see page 30) and buff the excess oxidation with steel wool. Tumble to work-harden and polish.

1   Measure the wire 7½" (19 cm) from one end and make a hairpin bend. Squeeze the bend flat with flat-nose pliers (**FIG. 1**).

2   Measure ⅞" (2.2 cm) from the bend on the longer wire and mark with a Sharpie. Insert the flat-nose

pliers between the wires, with the edge of the pliers on the mark. Bend the wire around the outside of the bottom jaw of the flat-nose pliers (**FIG. 2**). Squeeze the bend flat with the flat-nose pliers

3   Grasp the middle of the folds with flat-nose pliers, so the tail wires are

NAUTICAL KNOT

Inspired by nautical knots, this link combines two types of wire—twisted wire and round wire—to create a ropelike semblance.

fig. 1

fig. 2

fig. 3

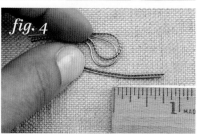

fig. 4

fig. 5

fig. 6

fig. 7

1 Straighten both pieces of wire and mark the midpoint of each wire with the Sharpie.

2 Grasp both wires on the mark with bail-forming pliers. Wrap the right-hand wires up and around the 8.5 mm barrel, pressing firmly to create a rounded shape. Try to keep the wires together, as they will shift (**FIG. 1**).

3 Turn the loop around so that the short wires point up and the longer wires are on the right-hand side (**FIG. 2**).

4 Insert the 6 mm barrel into the loop and wrap the longer wires tightly up and around the 8.5 mm barrel. The ends of the wire will point in opposite directions (**FIG. 3**).

5 Hold the wires together tightly and measure the tail wires ¾" (2 cm) beyond the top of the loop (**FIG. 4**). Trim the excess. Repeat on the opposite side.

6 Hold the wires firmly to maintain their shape, as they will tend to slide. With your fingers, bend one set of tail wires slightly so that it can be inserted into the opposite loop. Wrap the wires through and around the loop twice, pulling tightly with chain-nose pliers (**FIGS. 5 AND 6**). Reinsert the barrel of the bail-forming pliers and press the wires around the barrel to reshape if needed.

7 Repeat Steps 6 and 7 with the remaining set of tail wires. Trim both sets of wires on the back side and press down the cut ends with chain-nose pliers to secure. If needed, squeeze the wraps closer together with chain-nose pliers (**FIG. 7**).

8 Hammer the link on each side a few times with the rawhide mallet on the bench block, focusing on the wrapped sections.

9 Oxidize the link with a brass-darkening solution (see page 30) and buff the excess oxidation with steel wool. Tumble to work-harden and polish.

MATERIALS

8" (20.5 cm) of 16-gauge pure copper
wire

TOOLS

Chain-nose pliers

Flat-nose pliers

Round-nose pliers

Bail-forming pliers, 8.5 mm

Stepped pliers, 5 mm

Flush cutters

Chasing hammer

Steel bench block

Liver of sulfur

Steel wool, #0000

Rotary tumbler with mixed stainless-
steel shot

Ruler

FINISHED SIZE

⅜" × 1¼" (1 × 3.2 cm)

LEVEL OF DIFFICULTY

More challenging ●●●

TIP

*All you need to create
a sturdy, beautiful
wire bracelet are 5 or
6 interlocking links,
7mm jump rings,
and a clasp!*

OVER-UNDER

Strength meets style in this wire version of a square knot. Simple loops not only lock the link in place, but make forming connections a cinch.

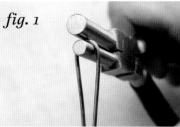

fig. 1

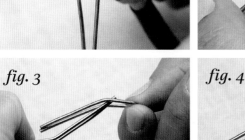

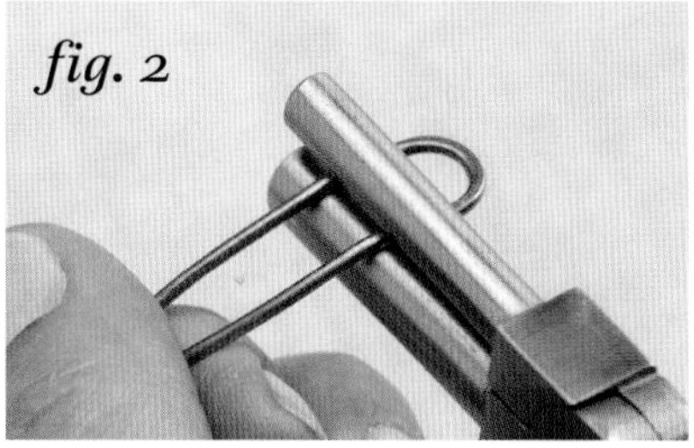

fig. 2

fig. 3

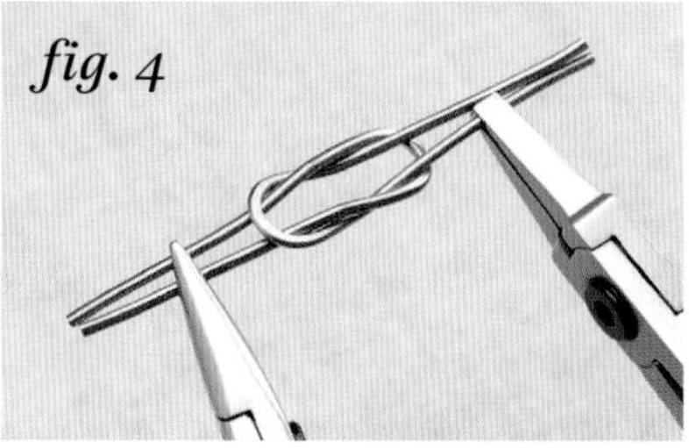

fig. 4

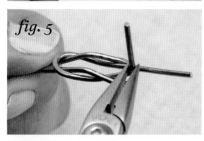

fig. 5

fig. 6

fig. 7

1 Flush-cut two 4" (10 cm) pieces of wire. Bend the middle of one piece of wire around the 6 mm barrel of the bail-forming pliers, bringing the tips together to form a teardrop shape (**FIG. 1**). Repeat with the second wire.

2 Hammer the curves of both wires with the chasing hammer on the bench block.

3 Grasp the wire ½" (1.3 cm) from the curve with the bail-forming pliers. Bend the wires slightly over the 8.5 mm barrel (**FIG. 2**). Repeat for the second wire.

4 Hold a curved wire in each hand with the tail ends pointing at each other. The curve of the left wire should be facing up and the curve of the right wire facing down. Insert the tails of the left wire into the curve of the right wire; then insert the tails of the right wire into the curve of the left wire (**FIG. 3**).

5 Slide the wires together slowly. Grasp the tail wires with flat- and chain-nose pliers and pull to tighten the "knot" (**FIG. 4**).

6 On one side of the link, trim the tail wires to ⅝" (1.5 cm) beyond the wire curve. Bend the two tail wires back 90° away from the curve, one at a time, with chain-nose pliers (**FIG. 5**).

7 Grasp both tail wires from Step 6 at the same time with the 5 mm barrel of the stepped pliers as shown. Roll the wires forward as far as you can to form simple loops (see page 22) (**FIG. 6**). Using chain-nose pliers, close each loop around the curve of the wire (**FIG. 7**). Squeeze the loops together so they are parallel. Repeat Steps 6 and 7 with the other tail wires.

8 Oxidize the link with liver of sulfur (see page 30) and buff the excess oxidation with steel wool. Tumble to work-harden and polish.

TIPS

Using flat-nose pliers, adjust the loops so they are on the same plane and lie flat.

Experiment with variations such as a twisted wire coil or mixing metals.

SPIRAL SWIRL

Texture, depth, and charm. This link has it all, including simple loops that make connections so easy.

fig. 1

fig. 2

fig. 3

fig. 4

fig. 5

fig. 6

fig. 7

fig. 8

fig. 9

1 Use the coiling tool to form a coil (see page 24) with the 22-gauge wire. Remove the coil from the mandrel and trim to 1⅝" (4.1 cm) (**FIG. 1**). Set the coil aside.

2 Flush-cut and file both ends of the 16-gauge wire. Make a small loop at one end of the wire with the tip of the round-nose pliers. Grasp the loop with flat-nose pliers and form a spiral with 4 revolutions. Flatten the spiral slightly with the chasing hammer on the bench block (**FIG. 2**).

3 Push the center of the spiral out with the round-nose pliers to add dimension (**FIG. 3**).

4 Slide the coil onto the tail of the 16-gauge wire and push it around the outer ring of the spiral, making a complete circle (**FIG. 4**).

5 Mark any excess coil with the Sharpie (**FIG. 5**). Remove the coil and trim the excess with flush cutters. Slide the coil back onto the spiral to form a full circle.

6 Where the coil ends meet, grasp the tail wire with the back of the round-nose pliers and wrap the wire tightly up and around the pliers, forming a loop (**FIG. 6**). Do not cut the wire.

7 Flip the link over to the back and, with your fingers, shape the wire into a curve underneath half of the coil (**FIG. 7**).

8 Measuring from the middle of the bottom of the link, trim the tail wire to ¾" (2 cm) (**FIG. 8**). Grasp the wire with the back of the round-nose pliers and roll the wire forward to form a simple loop (see page 22) (**FIG. 9**). Flatten both end loops slightly with the hammer and bench block.

9 Oxidize the link with liver of sulfur (see page 30) and buff the excess oxidation with steel wool. Tumble to work-harden and polish.

MATERIALS
15" (38 cm) of 18-gauge sterling silver–filled dead-soft wire

TOOLS
Chain-nose pliers

Flat-nose pliers

Long round-nose pliers

Flush cutters

Chasing hammer

Steel bench block

Sharpie

Liver of sulfur

Steel wool, #0000

Rotary tumbler with mixed stainless-steel shot

Ruler

FINISHED SIZE
¼" × 1⅝" (6 mm × 4.1 cm)

LEVEL OF DIFFICULTY
More challenging ●●●

SWIZZLE STICKS

Would you believe this link is created with one continuous piece of wire?
Add length and wound wire to your designs with this imaginative connector.

fig. 1

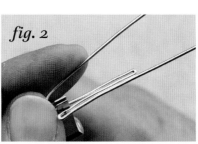

fig. 3

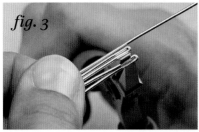

fig. 4

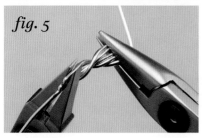

fig. 7

fig. 2

fig. 6

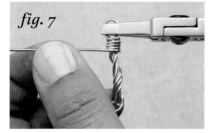

fig. 5

directions (**FIG. 3**). Squeeze the bend to flatten and align the wires.

4 Grasp the middle of the wires horizontally with flat-nose pliers and bend each tail wire down 90° against the folded edges (**FIG. 4**).

5 Grasp each folded end with pliers and rotate the pliers in opposite directions, twisting the entire wire bundle (**FIG. 5**). Once the desired amount of twist is achieved, squeeze the ends back together. The tail wires should still point in opposite directions.

6 Using the back of the long round-nose pliers, begin a wrapped loop (see page 23) with one tail wire (**FIG. 6**).

7 Wrap the tail 5 times around the twisted wires, keeping the wraps parallel (**FIG. 7**). Trim the wire tail and press down the cut end with chain-nose pliers to secure.

8 Repeat Steps 6 and 7, being sure to cover the folded end. Trim the wire on the same side of link as before.

9 Flatten the loops slightly with the chasing hammer on the bench block.

10 Oxidize the link with liver of sulfur (see page 30) and buff with steel wool. Tumble to work-harden and polish.

1 Measure 7½" (19 cm) from one end of the wire and make a hairpin bend. Squeeze the bend tightly with flat-nose pliers, so the wires are parallel (**FIG. 1**).

2 Mark the wires ⅞" (2.2 cm) from the bend with a Sharpie. Insert flat-nose pliers between the wires, with the edge of the pliers on the mark. Bend the wire over the flat-nose pliers and squeeze the bend to flatten and align the wires. Repeat with the other wire (**FIG. 2**).

3 Insert flat-nose pliers between the center bend and the longer wire. Make a fourth and final bend. The tail wires will point in opposite directions.

MATERIALS

12" (30.5 cm) of 18-gauge pure copper wire

12" (30.5 cm) of 22-gauge pure copper wire

3' (91.5 cm) of 24-gauge pure copper wire

TOOLS

Chain-nose pliers

Coiling tool or steel mandrel, 2 mm

Flush cutters

Toho seed bead tube (or 16 mm mandrel)

Chasing hammer

Rawhide mallet

Steel bench block

Liver of sulfur

Steel wool, #0000

Rotary tumbler with mixed stainless-steel shot

Ruler

FINISHED SIZE

1" (2.5 cm)

LEVEL OF DIFFICULTY

More challenging ●●●

TIP

Try mixing up the three types of metal to spice up your project. You can also customize this link by varying the diameter of the mandrel.

TWIST AGAIN

Three gauges of wire are twisted and coiled to form a hefty round link. Adding patina will give this link even more depth!

fig. 1

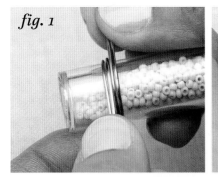
fig. 2

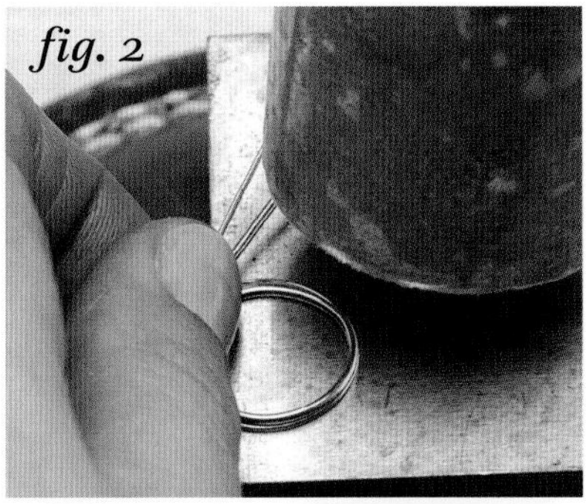

fig. 3

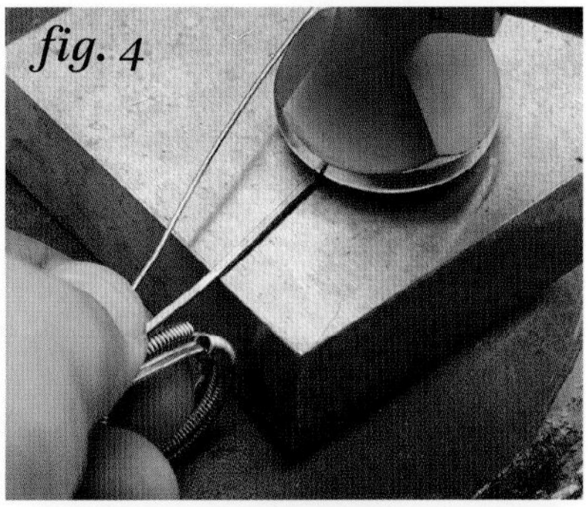

fig. 4

fig. 5

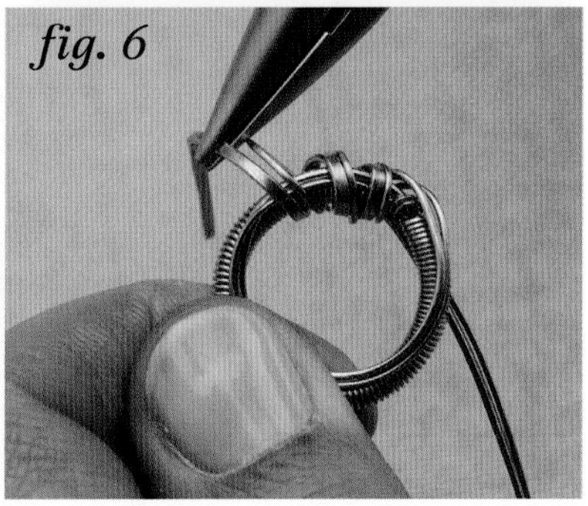

fig. 6

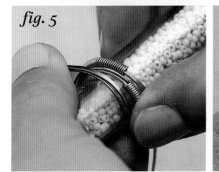

4 Slide the coil over both tail wires on one end (**FIG. 3**). Feed the coil around the circle, forming a coiled circle. The sets of tail wires will point in opposite directions.

5 Separate the 18-gauge tail ends slightly and flatten with the chasing hammer and bench block (**FIG. 4**).

6 Slide the circle back onto the seed bead tube and wrap one set of tail wires around the tube once, forming another circle beside the coiled circle. Pull the wires tightly as you form the circle (**FIG. 5**). Remove the tube, holding the circles in place to maintain their shape.

7 Begin wrapping one set of 18- and 22-gauge wires around the circle frame in a loose, random fashion. Use chain-nose pliers to pull the wires around individually—they will be stiff from work-hardening (**FIG. 6**).

8 Repeat Step 7 with the remaining set of tail wires, winding the wires around the circle frame in the opposite direction. Trim the wires on the inside of the link and press down with chain-nose pliers to secure.

9 Oxidize the link with liver of sulfur (see page 30) and buff the excess oxidation with steel wool. Tumble to work-harden and polish.

1 Use the 24-gauge copper wire and coiling tool to form a 2⅛" (5.4 cm) coil; set aside.

2 Place the seed bead tube on the middle of both the 18- and 22-gauge copper wires. Wrap both wires firmly around the tube until

the wires form a complete circle, with the tail ends pointing in opposite directions (**FIG. 1**).

3 Place the circle on the bench block and hammer with the rawhide mallet to reinforce the circular shape (**FIG. 2**).

WIRE LINKS IN DESIGN

Take a look at the many ways wire links can be used: as chain, decorative elements, bails, and as focals. I've been joined by a selection of accomplished artists to present wire links that are featured in fifteen jewelry designs. Each designer has shared her thoughts on what inspired her design, possible variations to consider, tips, and more. Use these projects and ideas as springboards to add both function and beauty to your original designs!

MATERIALS

12" (30.5 cm) of 16-gauge red brass wire

16" (40.6 cm) of 18-gauge red brass wire

21" (53.3 cm) of 18-gauge twisted red brass wire

6.8' (2.1 m) of 20-gauge red brass wire

4.25' (1.3 m) of 22-gauge twisted red brass wire

28" (71.1 cm) of .019" flexible beading wire

2 amazonite 12 × 7mm faceted pear beads

19 blue topaz 10 × 6mm faceted beads

8 lapis 10mm faceted round beads

11 kyanite 14 × 8mm oval beads

6 brass 2mm cubes

16 brass 7mm flower bead caps

2 brass 9mm flower bead caps

4 brass 4mm crimp covers

4 sterling silver 2mm crimp tubes

1 brass 1½" (3.8 cm) head pin

TOOLS

Chain-nose pliers

Flat-nose pliers

Round-nose pliers

Bail-forming pliers or steel mandrels, 6 mm and 8.5 mm

Stepped pliers or steel mandrel, 5 mm

Crimping pliers

Flush cutters

Wire cutters

Rawhide mallet

Steel bench block

Sharpie

Oxidizing solution (Novacan Black or JAX)

Steel wool, #0000

Rotary tumbler with mixed stainless-steel shot

Ruler

FINISHED LENGTH

19" (48.3 cm)

AFTERNOON IN ANNAPOLIS

CINDY WIMMER

Locals and tourists alike fill the downtown harbor in Annapolis to see the sailboats, enjoy the restaurants, and to stroll. There is something so charming about a port town, drawing all of us in. I met my husband in this town on my twenty-first birthday. We both come from Navy families, so it's no surprise that I enjoy nautical themes. I make my salute in this necklace, with a wire rope for a focal and chain made to resemble square knots.

FEATURED LINKS

Nautical Knot (page 84)
Owl Eyes (page 62)

1 Make an Owl Eyes link focal (see page 62) using 21" (53.3 cm) of 18-gauge twisted red brass wire and the 6 mm barrel of the bail-forming pliers. Leave enough of a gap in the final loop to be able to attach the necklace sections later. When finishing the link, rather than trimming the extra wire, wrap the tails around the center of the link an additional time.

2 Make 9 Nautical Knot links (see page 84) using the 20-gauge red brass wire and the 22-gauge twisted red brass wire. Set aside.

3 Make 19 jump rings (see page 25) using the 5 mm barrel of the stepped pliers and the 18-gauge plain (not twisted) red brass wire; set aside.

Make 5 jump rings using the 6 mm barrel of the bail-forming pliers and the 16-gauge wire. Open the 16-gauge jump rings and attach to one another to make an extender chain; set aside. Use the remaining 16-gauge wire to create a spiral S-hook clasp (see page 28).

4 Oxidize the jump rings, clasp, links, bead caps, and remaining length of 20-gauge wire (in a loose coil), using Novacan Black or JAX (see page 30). Buff the excess oxidization with steel wool. Place the jump rings, clasp, and links into the tumbler to polish.

5 Open three 5mm jump rings and attach one end of one Nautical Knot link to the outer loop on one side

of the Owl Eyes link focal; close the jump rings. To the other end of the Nautical Knot link, attach 3 additional Nautical Knot links in a chain and the hook clasp, using two 5mm jump rings between links. For the opposite side of the necklace, attach 5 Nautical Knot links in a chain using two 5mm jump rings between links. Attach one end of the extender chain to one end of the 5-Nautical Knot links chain. String a 2mm brass bead and 1 blue topaz bead onto a head pin and begin a wrapped loop (see page 23), attaching the loop to the other end of the extender chain before completing the wrap. Trim the excess wire and tuck in the tail with chain-nose pliers.

6 Cut 4" (10.2 cm) of 20-gauge wire and begin a wrapped loop on one end. Attach this loop to the outer loop on the other side of the Owl Eyes link focal; complete the wrapped loop. String one 7mm bead cap, 1 lapis bead, and another 7mm bead cap onto the wire; make a second wrapped loop. Make 6 more lapis bead units, attaching the last loop on each bead unit to the last loop on the previous unit. Make 1 more lapis bead unit, attaching one end to the previous bead unit and the other end to the last link on the 5-Nautical Knot links chain from Step 5.

7 Start the next bead strand on the right of the lapis bead chain. Cut 14" (35.6 cm) of flexible beading wire, string 1 crimp tube on one end and the outer loop of the Owl Eye link focal; pass the beading wire back through the tube and crimp. String 1 amazonite bead, one 9mm bead cap, 11 kyanite beads, one 9mm bead cap, and 1 amazonite bead. String 1 crimp tube and (to the right side of the lapis bead chain) the last link on the 5-Nautical Knot link chain. Note: The strands should be parallel, not twisted. Pass the beading wire back through the crimp tube, amazonite bead, and bead cap; pull the wire slightly to remove the excess slack and crimp.

8 Start the final strand on the left side of the lapis chain. Using the remaining 14" (35.6 cm) of beading wire, string 1 crimp tube and the outer loop of the Owl Eye link focal; pass back through the tube and crimp. String 3 blue topaz beads and one 2mm brass cube. Repeat this sequence another 5 times, omitting the final brass cube. String 1 crimp tube and (on the left side of the lapis chain), the last link of the 5-Nautical Knot link chain. All 3 strands should be parallel to each other, not twisted. Pass the beading wire back through the crimp tube and 1 blue topaz bead; pull the wire slightly to remove the excess slack and crimp. Cover all the crimps with crimp covers.

MATERIALS

Spool of 14-gauge pure copper wire, 32½" (82.5 cm) used

8' (2.43 m) of 22-gauge bronze wire

4 London blue topaz faceted nuggets

14 citrine faceted nuggets

1 brass scalloped collar blank, 4½" × 1" (11.5 × 2.5 cm)

TOOLS

Chain-nose pliers

Flat-nose pliers

Round-nose pliers

Metal hole-punch pliers, 1.8 mm

Nylon jaw bracelet-bending pliers

Steel mandrel, 10 mm

Flush cutters, heavy-duty

Chasing hammer

Texture hammer, double-faced (dimples/narrow striped)

Decorative metal stamps and brass hammer (optional)

Rawhide mallet

Steel bench block

Half-round file

Sanding pad, 320-grit

Renaissance Wax

Sharpie

Liver of sulfur

Steel wool, #0000

Cotton cloth, small piece

Rotary tumbler with mixed stainless-steel shot

Ruler

FINISHED LENGTH

16" (40.5 cm)

AMBER SKIES

DIANE COOK

In the deep south of Texas, the wide-open skies often come alive with shades of amber and blue at sunset. I wanted to evoke the beauty of those skies in this design. After I made the Little Orbits links using copper as the base and wrapping them loosely with bronze wire, the design came alive in my mind's eye. I added simple texture to a brass collar blank before deciding to use faceted citrine and London blue topaz nugget dangles, along with the gorgeous Little Orbits.

FEATURED LINK
Little Orbits (page 42)

1 Place the brass collar blank on the bench block and flatten it with the rawhide mallet. Use the dimple side of the texture hammer to texture the front of the collar. Add additional texture to the edges of the collar with the ball end of the chasing hammer. Use the bracelet-bending pliers to create a gentle bend in the collar, working from the middle toward one end and then repeat toward the other end.

2 Place dots on the lower scalloped edge of the collar with the Sharpie where the desired number of holes will be punched. Punch the holes with the hole-punch pliers (13 holes were made in this design). Turn the collar over and remove any burrs created by the punched holes with the half-round file.

3 Wind the copper wire into a loosely coiled spool; repeat for the bronze wire. Oxidize the collar and wire in liver of sulfur (see page 30); set the wire aside.

4 Remove the desired amount of patina on the collar by first sanding with the 320-grit sanding pad, then finish with steel wool. With a piece of soft cloth, rub Renaissance Wax sparingly onto the collar to seal the patina. Set the collar aside.

5 Using the 10 mm mandrel and spool of 14-gauge copper wire, make 16 jump rings (see page 25). Add texture to each jump ring as described in the Little Orbits link (see page 42) tutorial.

6 Make 1 Little Orbits link using 1 copper jump ring from Step 5 and two 4½" (11.5 cm) pieces of 22-gauge bronze wire.

7 Use 6 jump rings from Step 5 to make 6 more Little Orbits links, except this time wrap 4½" (11.5 cm) of bronze wire on only one side of each jump ring, covering the cut in the jump ring. These will be referred to as "Half Little Orbits links."

8 Use 3½" (9 cm) of 14-gauge copper wire to make an S-clasp (see page 28). Texture the clasp as you did the jump rings. Cut 6" (15 cm) of bronze wire and wrap the wire around the middle of the S-hook.

9 Buff the excess oxidation from the jump rings, links, and S-clasp with steel wool. Place the components in the tumbler for 1½ hours to work-harden and polish.

10 Cut 6" (15 cm) of bronze wire and begin a wrapped loop (see page 23) on one end of the wire. Attach the loop to the last punched hole on the bottom of one end of the collar before completing the wrap. Begin a second wrapped loop and attach it to 1 Half Little Orbits link before completing the wrap. Repeat this step on the opposite side of the collar.

11 Cut 6" (15 cm) of bronze wire and begin a wrapped loop on one end. Skip a hole in the collar from the previous hole, attach the loop, and complete the wrap. String a citrine nugget onto the wire and begin a second wrapped loop. Attach the loop to 1 Half Little Orbits link and complete the wrap. Repeat this step on the opposite side of the collar.

12 Repeat Step 11, attaching a topaz nugget and 1 Half Little Orbits link to each side of the collar.

13 Cut 6" (15 cm) of bronze wire and begin a wrapped loop on one end. Attach the loop to the center hole in the collar and complete the wrap. String a topaz nugget onto the wire and begin a second wrapped loop. Attach the Little Orbits link to the loop and complete the wrap.

14 Cut 6" (15 cm) of bronze wire and flatten ¼" (6 mm) on one end with a hammer on the bench block. Grasp the hammered end with the tip of the round-nose pliers and form a small loop. String a topaz nugget onto the wire, sliding it down to the

hammered loop. Begin a wrapped loop just above the topaz nugget, attaching the loop to the bottom of the Little Orbits link from Step 13; complete the wrap. Repeat this step, attaching a citrine nugget on either side of the topaz nugget.

15 Cut 18" (45.5 cm) of bronze wire. Measure 2" (5 cm) from one end of the wire and begin a wrapped loop. Slide 3 citrine nuggets onto the long wire and begin a second wrapped loop, attaching the second loop to the premade hole on one end of the collar. Wrap the long wire snugly up and around each of the nuggets, then once around the first loop. Wrap the long wire back down and around each of the nuggets again, then wrap the tail around the second loop, completing the wrap; trim the tail and tuck in the end with chain-nose pliers. Complete the wrap around the first loop, trim the excess wire, and tuck in the tail. Repeat this step on the opposite end of the collar.

16 Open 1 jump ring from Step 5 and attach it to the free loop on 1 citrine nugget unit from Step 15. Repeat on the other citrine nugget unit.

17 Cut 6" (15 cm) of bronze wire and begin a wrapped loop on one end. Attach the loop to 1 jump ring from Step 16, then complete the wrap. String a citrine nugget onto the wire and attach it to another jump ring with a wrapped loop. Repeat this step on the other side of the collar.

18 Repeat Step 17, attaching another citrine nugget and jump ring to each side of the collar. Connect 2 more jump rings together in a chain, attaching one to the S-hook clasp and the other to the jump ring on one end of the necklace. Open the remaining jump ring and attach it to the last jump ring on the other end of the necklace.

BUZZ ME IN

KERRY BOGERT

MATERIALS

- 10½' (3.2 m) of 16-gauge sterling silver dead-soft wire
- 6½' (2 m) of .019" flexible beading wire
- 14 sterling silver 2mm crimp tubes
- 200 size 8° blue seed beads
- 300 size 8° purple seed beads
- 100 size 8° green seed beads
- 100 size 8° purple-lined clear purple seed beads
- 24mm turquoise lampwork glass hollow bead
- 19mm blue swirl lampwork glass button with loop shank

TOOLS

- Chain-nose pliers
- Flat-nose pliers
- Round-nose pliers
- Crimping pliers
- Flush cutters
- Sharpie (or 12 mm mandrel)
- Flat hand file
- Chasing hammer
- Rawhide mallet
- Steel bench block
- Liver of sulfur
- Rotary tumbler with mixed stainless-steel shot
- Ruler

FINISHED LENGTH

20" (51 cm)

If color has energy, there is something kinetic and electric about blue. This necklace pairs a couple of curvy links that remind one of transistors and radio frequencies. Imagine ringing a doorbell and being able to see that little jolt that runs from the button to the bell. It's been captured visually in this colorful design.

FEATURED LINKS

Beehive (page 54)
SnoCone (page 64)

1 Make 8 Beehive links (see page 54). Use chain-nose pliers to open the simple loop (see page 22) on one end of a Beehive link as you would a jump ring and connect it to the simple loop of another Beehive link; close the loop. Repeat until you have connected all 8 links. Set aside.

2 Make 2 SnoCone links (see page 64) using the 16-gauge sterling silver wire. Set aside.

3 Cut 8" (20.5 cm) of 16-gauge wire and slide the lampwork glass hollow bead onto the wire. With about 1½" (3.8 cm) of wire sticking out one side of the bead, fold both wires up and around the bead, preparing to make a briolette wrapped loop. Crisscross the wires and wrap the short wire once around the longer wire; trim the short tail.

4 Using 5¼" (13.5 cm) of 16-gauge wire, make a large spiral as you did in Step 2 for the SnoCone link. String the spiral onto the long wire from Step 3 and form a large wrapped loop (using the Sharpie as a mandrel for the loop) locking the spiral in place; trim the excess wire and tuck in the tail with chain-nose pliers.

5 Hammer the loop of the pendant flat with the chasing hammer on the bench block. Be careful to keep the lampwork bead out of the way to prevent damaging it with the hammer. Set aside.

6 Cut seven 11" (28 cm) lengths of flexible beading wire. String a crimp tube onto one end of one beading wire, pass the wire around the bottom loop of a SnoCone link, and back through the crimp tube; crimp. String 100 seed beads onto the wire and crimp the other end of the strand to the bottom loop of the other SnoCone link. Repeat, attaching a total of 7 beaded strands to each SnoCone link.

7 Using chain-nose pliers, open the simple loop on top of one of the SnoCone links and connect it to an end loop on the Beehive link chain and the loop on the lampwork pendant bail; close the loop.

8 Open the simple loop on the other end of the Beehive link chain and connect it to the shank of the lampwork button; close the loop. This will become the catch for the clasp.

9 With the remaining 16-gauge wire, make a simple S-clasp (see page 28) and attach it to the free simple loop on the other SnoCone link.

10 Oxidize the necklace in liver of sulfur (see page 30) and tumble for about 1 hour. To achieve a deep gunmetal color, do not polish the necklace with steel wool before tumbling.

MATERIALS

5 labradorite 5mm faceted rondelles

1 citrine 8mm faceted nugget

1 carnelian 8 × 12mm oval bead

1 aquamarine 5mm faceted rondelle

16 turquoise 2mm heishi beads

6 sterling silver 3mm faceted nugget beads

1 copper 7 × 12mm oval stamping blank charm with loop

1 copper 20mm dotted circle component

16½" (42 cm) of 16-gauge pure copper wire

11" (28 cm) of 24-gauge sterling silver–filled wire

41" (104 cm) of 7-ply, chocolate brown waxed Irish linen

1 silver 15mm hook clasp

1 silver 5 × 11mm double-loop eye

1 copper 2mm crimp tube

2 sterling silver 3mm crimp tubes

TOOLS

Chain-nose pliers

Flat-nose pliers

Round-nose pliers

Bail-forming pliers or steel mandrel, 6 mm

Flush cutters

Sharpie

Scissors

2 mm metal lowercase alphabet stamp set

Brass stamping hammer

Chasing hammer

Steel bench block

Tape measure

Liver of sulfur

Steel wool, #0000

Polishing cloth

Rotary tumbler with mixed stainless-steel shot

Ruler

FINISHED LENGTH

17" (43 cm)

CREATE YOUR DREAM

TRACY STATLER

I wanted to use the Lightbulb links in an atypical way, setting three of them off individually instead of connecting one to the other. Going for a softer, less industrial feel, I created a collection of gemstone charms. The waxed Irish linen cording helps to further soften the look. The assembled piece reminded me of a modern dream catcher, so I added the stamped "dream" charm—to gently encourage you to dream and look at things in new and interesting ways!

FEATURED LINK
Lightbulb (page 40)

1 Make 3 Lightbulb links (see page 40) using the 16-gauge pure copper wire; set aside.

2 Cut 3" (7.5 cm) of 24-gauge wire and make a small simple loop (see page 22) on one end with the tip of the round-nose pliers. String 5 labradorite rondelles and 1 copper crimp tube, sliding them down against the simple loop. Begin a wrapped loop (see page 23), attaching the loop to the left side of the copper circle component before completing the wrap. Trim the excess wire and press the tail down with chain-nose pliers. Repeat this step, stringing the aquamarine, citrine, and carnelian beads together and attaching the loop to the circle component, to the right of the labradorite dangle.

3 Cut 5" (12.5 cm) of 24-gauge wire and create a small simple loop at one end. String all the turquoise heishi beads onto the wire, sliding them down against the simple loop. Pass the other end of the wire through the simple loop forming a teardrop shape with the beads. Begin a wrapped loop, attaching the loop to the right of the previous dangle on the circle component. Complete the wrap, wrapping the wire until the small loop is covered completely. Flush-cut the excess wire and press the tail down with chain-nose pliers.

4 Open the loop on the long end of one of the Lightbulb links with pliers as you would a jump ring. Attach the link to the circle component, to the right of the previous dangle; close the loop.

5 Using metal stamps and the brass hammer on the bench block, stamp the word "dream" on the middle of the oval blank charm. Texture the blank with the ball end of the chasing hammer.

6 Open the loops on the long ends of the two remaining Lightbulb links. Slide the "dream" charm onto one of the links, pushing it around to the right side of the link. Cut 1" (2.5 cm) of waxed linen and tie a knot under the charm to hold it in place; trim the waxed linen tails. Attach this link to the right side of the circle component, to the right of the dangles; close the loop. Attach the other link to the left side of the circle component, to the left of the dangles; close the loop.

7 Cut the remaining waxed linen into two 20" (51 cm) lengths. Fold one length in half and attach it with a lark's head knot to the short loop on one of the Lightbulb links added in Step 6. Repeat with the other length of waxed linen and the second Lightbulb link.

8 Starting on the right side of the necklace (the side with the "dream" charm), measure 1" (2.5 cm) from the lark's head knot on the right (outer) strand of waxed linen and tie a slipknot. String 1 silver nugget, slide it down to the knot, and tie another slipknot on the other side of the silver nugget. Measure 2" (5 cm) from the last knot and tie another knot. String a silver nugget and tie a knot. Make sure the knots

TIPS

To form a lark's head knot, fold the waxed linen in half. String the folded end of the linen through the hole of the circle component. Pass the free ends of the linen through the linen loop and tighten.

If you desire an antiqued-look, oxidize the silver wire, Lightbulb links, hook clasp, silver nugget beads, and stamped "dream" charm with liver of sulfur gel (see page 30) prior to assembling. Buff the excess oxidization with steel wool and polish with a polishing cloth.

are tight and snug against the beads. Measure 2" (5 cm) from the lark's head knot on the left (inner) strand and tie a knot. String a silver nugget and tie another knot.

9 Repeat Step 8 for the left side of the necklace, with the left (outer) strand matching the right (outer) strand in Step 8, and the right (inner) strand on the left side of the necklace matching the left (inner) strand in Step 8.

10 Straighten the waxed linen strands so they are not tangled. Slide a 3mm crimp tube over both waxed linen strands on each side of the necklace, sliding it down a few inches. Measure the desired length for the necklace. String both tails on one side of the necklace through the small loop on the hook and pass back through the crimp tube; flatten the crimp with chain-nose pliers to secure. Repeat, adding the eye to the other side of the necklace. Trim the excess waxed linen.

MATERIALS

20" (51 cm) of 24-gauge silver-filled wire

7" (18 cm) of 26-gauge sterling silver half-hard wire

Spool of 12-gauge pure copper wire

2 silver 10mm potato pearls

4 copper 4mm nugget beads

10 sterling silver 2mm round nugget beads

8" (20.5 cm) of 1.5 mm brown leather cording

1 sterling silver crimp-end hook-and-eye clasp

TOOLS

Chain-nose pliers

Flat-nose pliers

Round-nose pliers

Stepped pliers or steel mandrel, 7 mm

Nylon jaw bracelet-bending pliers

Flush cutters, heavy-duty

Flat hand file

Chasing hammer

Steel bench block

Scissors

Two-hole screw-down punch, 1.6 mm

Sharpie

G-S Hypo Cement

Liver of sulfur

Steel wool, #0000

Polishing cloth

Rotary tumbler with mixed stainless-steel shot

Ruler

FINISHED LENGTH

7½" (19 cm)

DOWN TO EARTH

TRACY STATLER

The Stitched Figure-Eight link is the perfect focal point for a bracelet. I love the combination of oxidized copper and silver, so I chose a neutral color palette to complement it and added silver pearls to contrast with the hard metals. Rustic brown leather cord completes the earthy look.

FEATURED LINK
Stitched Figure Eight (page 68)

1 Make 1 Stitched Figure-Eight link (see page 68). Place the link in the bracelet-bending pliers and squeeze gently to form a slight curve; set aside.

2 Flush-cut 10" (25.5 cm) of 24-gauge wire. Measure 2" (6.4 cm) from one end and begin a wrapped loop (see page 23) with the middle of the round-nose pliers, forming a 4 mm loop. Attach the loop to one side of the Stitched Figure-Eight link and complete the wrap. Tuck in the wire tail with chain-nose pliers.

3 String 1 copper nugget, 1 silver pearl, and 1 copper nugget onto the other end of the wire. Begin a second 4 mm wrapped loop, wrapping 2 times, but do not cut the tail. Crisscross the tail over the front of the pearl unit at a diagonal and wrap the wire under the first loop, then bring the wire back toward the second loop, crossing over the other wire on the front and forming an X. Wrap the tail around the second loop a few times and trim the excess wire. Tuck in the tail with the chain-nose pliers.

4 Repeat Steps 2 and 3 on the other side of the Stitched Figure-Eight link.

5 Cut 4" (10 cm) of leather cord. Fold the cord in half and squeeze the bend to maintain the fold. Thread one end of the cord through one loop on the end of one pearl unit. Slide the wire loop down to the bend. Cut 3" (7.5 cm) of 24-gauge wire and wrap once around the cords, near the bend, to secure; tighten the wire with flat-nose pliers, but do not cut the wire. String 3 silver nugget rounds onto the wire, making sure they are on the front of the cords; wrap the wire around the cords. Repeat, stringing 2 silver nugget rounds. Wrap the wire around again, making a fourth pass, then gently squeeze the wire flat with flat-nose pliers. Trim the excess wire and tuck in the tail with chain-nose pliers. Repeat this step for the other side of the bracelet.

6 Apply G-S Hypo Cement to the tips of the leather cording (about ¼" [6 mm], the amount of leather that will fit inside the crimp-end clasp). Place the ends of each leather cord section into each of the crimp-end clasps. Be careful not to twist or cross the leather cords. Gently crimp the clasp around the leather cords with flat-nose pliers. Quickly wipe off any extra glue that may have squeezed out while crimping.

7 Let dry for at least 30 minutes.

TIP

Oxidize the silver wire and crimp-end clasp with liver of sulfur (see page 30) prior to assembling if you prefer an antiqued finish. Buff the excess oxidization with steel wool and polish with a polishing cloth.

ODE TO DOWNTON ABBEY

MATERIALS

50 coin pearl 12 × 14–16mm teardrops

4 mother-of-pearl 12mm carved rose beads

82 mother-of-pearl 4mm faceted rounds

16' (4.9 m) of 18-gauge red brass wire

2 brass 3½" (9 cm) antique buckle connecting halves

20 brass 4mm bead caps

4 sterling silver 2mm crimp tubes

4 brass 4mm crimp covers

4' (1.2 m) of antique bronze-colored .019" flexible beading wire

TOOLS

Chain-nose pliers

Flat-nose pliers

Round-nose pliers

Bail-forming pliers or steel mandrels, 6 mm and 8.5 mm

Crimping pliers

Flush cutters

Flat hand file

Chasing hammer

Rawhide mallet

Steel bench block

Sharpie

Antiquing solution (Patina Black for Solder or JAX)

Steel wool, #0000

Rotary tumbler with mixed stainless-steel shot

Ruler

FINISHED LENGTH

17" (43 cm)

CINDY WIMMER

When I stumbled upon this antique belt buckle at a flea market, I immediately knew that it would make a fantastic focal for a necklace. By adding vintage components that have been selected with care, you can add nostalgia and even intrigue to your jewelry. Strands of pearls further this romantic notion, while the link chain draws the eye from the buckle and back around again. Suit your fancy by wearing with the buckle closure at the side or at the back of the neck.

FEATURED LINK
Triple Loop (page 70)

1 Make 15 Triple Loop links (see page 70) with 18-gauge red brass wire and set aside.

2 Make 14 jump rings (see page 25) using the 6 mm barrel of the bail-forming pliers and the 18-gauge wire; the outer diameter (OD) of these jump rings will be 9mm. Repeat with the 8.5 mm

barrel of the bail-forming pliers, making 4 additional jump rings that are 11mm in outer diameter.

3 Oxidize the jump rings and Triple Loop links with the antiquing solution (see page 30). Buff the excess oxidation with steel wool. Tumble the jump rings and links for 1 hour.

4 Open one 9mm jump ring and attach it to one end of one Triple Loop link; close the jump ring. Repeat, attaching all the remaining Triple Loop links with 9mm jump rings to form a chain. Open one 11mm jump ring and attach it to one end of the chain and the outer edge of one buckle half; close the

jump ring. Repeat, attaching the other end of the chain to the outer edge of the other buckle half.

5 Cut 24" (61 cm) of flexible beading wire. Onto the end of the wire, string 1 crimp tube and one 11mm jump ring on one buckle half. Pass the wire tail back through the crimp tube and crimp with crimping pliers. String 1 bead cap, 1 mother-of-pearl round, 1 bead cap, and 8 mother-of-pearl rounds; repeat 8 times. String a final bead cap, mother-of-pearl round, and bead cap. String 1 crimp tube and the 11mm jump ring on the other buckle half and pass the wire back through the crimp tube; crimp. Trim the excess wire and cover the crimps with crimp covers.

6 Attach the remaining two 11mm jump rings to the outer edge on each buckle half. Attach one end of the remaining 24" (61 cm) length of beading wire to one of these jump rings using a crimp tube, as in Step 5. String 2 carved rose beads, all 50 teardrop coin pearls, and 2 more carved rose beads. Attach the end of the flexible beading wire to the other jump ring added in this step using a crimp tube. Trim the excess wire and cover the crimps with crimp covers.

TIP

Search for antique buckles both online and at local antique malls and flea markets. Modern alternatives from fabric store notions sections can be used as well.

MATERIALS

2½" × 1½" (6.5 × 3.8 cm) green/brown/light green ceramic gingko leaf pendant

6 mottled green/blue/ivory 22mm Kazuri ceramic coins

4 ivory-and-gold patterned 12mm vintage Lucite rounds

4' (1.2 m) of 16-gauge pure copper wire

30" (76 cm) of 18-gauge pure copper wire

14 copper 10mm 18-gauge jump rings

1 copper S-hook clasp of your choice

3" (7.5 cm) dark green/burgundy sari silk ribbon

TOOLS

Chain-nose pliers

Flat-nose pliers

Round-nose pliers

Stepped pliers or steel mandrels, 2 mm and 5 mm

Sharpie (or 12 mm mandrel)

Flush cutters

Flat hand file

Chasing hammer

Rawhide mallet

Steel bench block

Liver of sulfur (optional)

Steel wool, #0000 (optional)
Rotary tumbler with mixed stainless-steel shot

Ruler

FINISHED LENGTH

23" (58.5 cm)

GINGKO

LORI ANDERSON

The perfect necklace for nature lovers! The ceramic gingko leaf offers a dramatic backdrop for three special links. The Whirligig link acts as a bail for the sari silk ribbon, and the Springboard and Engagement Ring links add texture to the ivory, green, and blue Kazuri coin beads. Try this combination to feature your favorite handmade pendant and complementary beads!

FEATURED LINKS

Springboard (page 66)
Whirligig (page 50)
Engagement Ring (page 38)

1 Make 3 Springboard links, 1 Whirligig link, and 3 Engagement Ring links with 16-gauge copper wire (see pages 66, 50, and 38); set aside. If desired, oxidize the links, jump rings, and 18-gauge wire with liver of sulfur (see page 30). Buff the excess oxidization with steel wool. Tumble the links to work-harden and polish.

2 String the ribbon through the center hole in the pendant and attach it to the U portion of the Whirligig link using an overhand knot. Be careful to leave a little leeway between the knot and the pendant.

3 Cut six 3" (7.5 cm) pieces of 18-gauge wire. Form a wrapped loop (see page 23) on one end of one wire, string 1 ceramic coin, and form a second wrapped loop on the other end. Repeat with 4 more ceramic coins for a total of 5 coin units. Repeat, making 1 Lucite round unit. Set aside.

4 Starting on the left-hand side of the necklace, open 2 jump rings and attach the left hole of the Whirligig link to one loop on 1 coin unit; close the jump rings.

5 Open the bottom simple loop of 1 Springboard link and attach it to the free loop of the coin unit just added; close the loop. Open the top simple loop of the Springboard link and attach it to one loop of another coin unit; close the loop. Repeat once more. You will now have 1 coin unit/Springboard link/coin unit/Springboard link/coin unit section.

6 Open 2 jump rings and attach the free loop on the last coin unit added to one loop on another coin unit. Open 2 jump rings and connect the free loop of the last

8 Cut 3" (7.5 cm) of 18-gauge wire and make a wrapped loop on one end of the wire. Open the top simple loop of the Springboard link and attach the wrapped loop; close the loop. String the last ceramic coin onto the wire and begin a second wrapped loop, attaching the loop to the "ring" part of 1 Engagement Ring link before completing the wrap.

9 Cut 3" (7.5 cm) of 18-gauge wire and make a wrapped loop on one end. Open 2 jump rings and connect the wrapped loop to the simple loops of the Engagement Ring link; close the jump rings. String 1 Lucite round onto the wire and begin a second wrapped loop, attaching the loop to the "ring" part of another Engagement Ring link before completing the wrap. Repeat once.

10 Cut 3" (7.5 cm) of 18-gauge wire and make a wrapped loop on one end. String 1 Lucite round and make a second wrapped loop that is large enough for the S-hook to fit through. Open 2 jump rings and attach the small loop on the Lucite unit to the simple loops on the last Engagement Ring link from Step 9; close the jump rings. Hammer the large loop on the Lucite unit with the rawhide mallet on the bench block to work-harden.

coin unit to one loop of 1 Lucite round unit from Step 3; close the jump rings. Attach the free loop of the Lucite round unit to the base of the S-hook clasp.

7 Starting on the right-hand side of the necklace, open 2 jump rings and connect the right hole in the Whirligig link and one loop of a coin unit; close the jump rings. Open the bottom simple loop of the remaining Springboard link and attach it to the free loop of the coin unit just added; close the loop.

MATERIALS

12" (30.5 cm) of 16-gauge sterling silver dead-soft wire

3' (.91 m) of 18-gauge sterling silver dead-soft wire

3' (.91 m) of 22-gauge sterling silver wire

9' (2.7 m) of 24-gauge sterling silver wire

1 turquoise 15mm carved melon bead

1 lapis 12 × 10mm Tibetan capped round bead

1 coral 16 × 13mm Tibetan capped round bead

1 amber 19 × 14mm Tibetan capped oval bead

1 kyanite 18 × 10mm tube bead

1 sterling silver 17 × 14mm Bali bead

1 hill tribe 11 × 11mm flower-and-leaf charm

2 sterling silver 9mm Bali daisy spacers

2 silver 13mm pancake spacer beads

1 sterling silver 2" (5 cm) head pin

2 silver 3mm twisted crimp tubes

2 sterling silver 4mm crimp covers

15" (38 cm) of .019" flexible beading wire

TOOLS

Bail-forming pliers, 6 mm

Chain-nose pliers

Flat-nose pliers

Round-nose pliers

Coiling tool or steel mandrel, 2 mm

Toho seed bead tube (or 16 mm mandrel)

Flush cutters

Flat hand file

Crimping tool (optional)

Chasing hammer

Rawhide mallet

Steel bench block

Sharpie (or 12 mm mandrel)

Liver of sulfur

Steel wool, #0000

Rotary tumbler with mixed stainless-steel shot

Ruler

FINISHED LENGTH

8" (20.5 cm)

GRAND BAZAAR

CINDY WIMMER

Multiple wire gauges entwine to form the Twist Again link, giving each link the look of a handwoven basket rim. The wire links are joined by an exotic blend of colorful beads. While I was designing this bracelet, a bustling marketplace came to mind. I imagined crowds of international traders at the famed Grand Bazaar of Istanbul. There, baskets are filled with all sorts of colorful textiles, spices, and pottery. Capture a miniature marketplace with this rendition for your wrist.

FEATURED LINK
Twist Again (page 92)

1 Make 3 Twist Again links (see page 92). Set aside.

2 Make 4 figure-eight connector links: these will serve as jump rings. Flush-cut four 1¾" (4.5 cm) pieces of 16-gauge wire. Grasp the end of one piece of wire with bail-forming pliers and roll the wire forward around the 6 mm barrel until the wire touches itself. Repeat on the other end of the wire, rolling the wire forward in the opposite direction.

3 Open one loop of a figure-eight link with chain-nose pliers as you would a jump ring and attach it to one Twist Again link; close the loop. Open the loop on the other side of the figure-eight link and at-tach it to another Twist Again link; close the loop. Repeat, attaching a second figure-eight link to these Twist Again links. Attach another Twist Again link to the previous one with a pair of figure-eight links. Set aside.

4 Using the back of the round-nose pliers, make 2 jump rings (see page 23) with 16-gauge wire. Make an S-hook clasp (see page 28) with the remaining 16-gauge wire.

5 Oxidize the Twist Again links, jump rings, crimp covers, and clasp in liver of sulfur (see page 30). Buff the excess oxidization with steel wool. Place all the components except the crimp covers in the tumbler to polish for about 1 hour.

6 Attach 1 jump ring to one of the end Twist Again links. String 1 crimp tube and the jump ring onto the end of the beading wire; pass the wire back through the crimp tube and squeeze the tube tightly with chain-nose pliers to secure.

7 String the following onto the beading wire: coral bead, pancake bead, kyanite bead, pancake bead, Bali bead, Bali spacer, turquoise melon bead, Bali spacer, amber bead, and crimp tube. Pass the wire through the clasp and back through the crimp tube and amber bead. Pull the wire to remove the excess slack. Secure the crimp by squeezing it tightly with chain-nose pliers. Trim the beading wire. Cover crimps with crimp covers using the crimping tool.

8 String the lapis bead onto the head pin and form a wrapped loop. Trim the excess wire and tuck in the tail with chain-nose pliers. Open the remaining jump ring and attach the wrapped loop, charm, and base loop of the S-hook clasp; close the jump ring.

MATERIALS

3¼" (8.5 cm) of 16-gauge sterling silver dead-soft wire

5½" (1.5 m) of 18-gauge sterling silver dead-soft wire

18" (45.5 cm) of 20-gauge sterling silver half-hard wire

28 sterling silver 18-gauge 5.3 × 4.3mm oval jump rings

1 vintage 2" × 3" (5 × 7.5 cm) art deco brooch

2 crystal/silver 6mm rondelles

4 antiqued 5 × 10mm bezel-set rhinestone connectors

1 rhinestone 14mm octagonal dangle

TOOLS

Chain-nose pliers

Flat-nose pliers

Round-nose pliers

Bail-forming pliers or steel mandrel, 6 mm and 8.5 mm

Metal hole-punch pliers, 1.8 mm

Flush cutters

Wire cutters, heavy-duty

Half-round file

Rawhide mallet

Chasing hammer

Steel bench block

Safety glasses

Sharpie (optional)

Steel wool, #0000

Sanding pad, 320-grit

Liver of sulfur

Rotary tumbler with mixed stainless-steel shot

Ruler

FINISHED LENGTH

19" (48.5 cm)

GREEN WITH INFINITY

DIANE COOK

The Double Infinity link beckoned me to dive into my stash of vintage brooches. I found a gorgeous art deco piece I picked up in Austin, Texas, at my favorite antiques shop on South Congress called Uncommon Objects. Because the center glass piece of the brooch is green, it became Green with Infinity!

FEATURED LINK
Double Infinity (page 78)

1 Make 11 Double Infinity links (see page 78).

2 To make the S-clasp, slightly flatten both ends of the 16-gauge wire with the chasing hammer on the steel bench block. Use the tip of the round-nose pliers to make small loops, facing opposite directions, on each end of the wire. With the 8.5 mm barrel of the bail-forming pliers, grasp one end of the wire just below the small loop, with the loop facing you, and roll the pliers forward until the loop touches the straight wire; repeat on the other end of the wire. Use the chasing hammer and steel bench block to flatten the curves of the clasp and set aside.

3 Oxidize the links, jump rings, S-clasp, crystal/silver rondelles, and the 20-gauge wire with liver of sulfur (see page 30). Buff the excess oxidization with steel wool. Tumble the links, jump rings, and clasp for 1 hour to work-harden and polish.

4 Using the heavy-duty wire cutters and, wearing safety glasses, carefully cut off the pin back on the brooch. File any sharp burrs that remain with the flat side of the file and use the sanding pad for a smooth finish.

5 Using the hole-punch pliers, punch 1 hole on each side on the top of the brooch, and 1 hole in the bottom center of the brooch. Turn the brooch over and smooth the back of the holes with the half-round side of the file.

6 Cut three 6" (15 cm) pieces of 20-gauge wire. Begin a wrapped loop (see page 23) on one end of

one wire, attaching the loop to a top hole in the brooch before completing the wrap. String 1 crystal/silver rondelle onto the wire and begin a second wrapped loop, attaching it to one loop on 1 rhinestone connector before finishing the wrap. Repeat this step with another 6" (15 cm) piece of wire on the other side of the brooch.

7 Begin a wrapped loop on one end of the remaining 6" (15 cm) wire from Step 6. Attach the loop to the bottom hole on the brooch and complete the wrap. String the loop on the octagonal dangle onto the wire and complete a second wrapped loop, wrapping the wire on top of the first wraps. Trim the excess wire and tuck in the tail with chain-nose pliers.

8 On the right side of the necklace, use 1 jump ring to attach one side of a Double Infinity link to the free loop on the rhinestone connector. Use 1 jump ring to attach the other side of the Double Infinity link to one loop on another rhinestone connector. Connect 6 Double Infinity links together in a chain, using 2 jump rings between each link. Use 1 jump ring to connect one end of the chain to the free loop on the last rhinestone connector added.

9 Repeat Step 8 on the left side of the necklace, except use 5 Double Infinity links for the chain instead of 6, and use 2 jump rings to attach the S-clasp to the free end of the chain.

MAGICIAN'S RINGS

MATERIALS

24" (61 cm) of 18-gauge sterling silver–filled dead-soft wire

8" (20.5 cm) of 20-gauge sterling silver–filled dead-soft wire

6" (15 cm) of 28-gauge turquoise anodized copper wire

2 lime green 6.7mm lampwork glass rondelles

2 orange and blue 14.4mm lampwork glass coin 20-gauge copper head pins

TOOLS

Chain-nose pliers

Round-nose pliers

Flush cutters

Flat hand file

Sharpie (or 12 mm mandrel)

Chasing hammer

Steel bench block

Liver of sulfur

Steel wool, #0000

Polishing cloth

Rotary tumbler with mixed stainless-steel shot

Ruler

FINISHED LENGTH

3¼" (8.5 cm), including the ear wire

KERRY BOGERT

When I was a little girl, I often wondered how in the world a magician was able to make his magic solid rings go together and come apart. It was an illusion that stumped me for years. Now, as an adult and wire artist to boot, I've figured things out, and I can work a little magic of my own with wire rings. The Classic Hoop links interlock and are highlighted by brightly colored glass dangles in these fun, playful earrings.

FEATURED LINK
Classic Hoop (page 36)

1 Make 2 Classic Hoop links (see page 36).

2 String 1 lampwork rondelle onto 1 lampwork coin head pin. Using round-nose pliers, begin a wrapped loop (see page 23) above the rondelle. Attach the head-pin loop to one small wrapped loop on one end of a Classic Hoop link. Wrap the head-pin loop closed in a chunky wrap style—wrapping the wire on top of previous wraps. Trim the excess wire and tuck in the tail with chain-nose pliers.

3 Make the ear wires. Cut 4" (10 cm) of 20-gauge wire. Using round-nose pliers, begin a wrapped loop about 2" (5 cm) from one end of the wire. Attach this loop to the free small wrapped loop at the opposite end of the Classic Hoop link in Step 2; complete the wrap. Using the Sharpie as a mandrel, bend the straight part of the 20-gauge wire over the Sharpie into a hook-shaped ear wire. Trim the wire tail so it lines up with the bottom of the loop on the ear wire. Grasp the tip of the tail with chain-nose pliers and make a small bend upward. File the end of the ear wire smooth.

Flatten the arch of the ear wire with the chasing hammer on the bench block. Repeat to make a second ear wire.

5 Cut 3" (7.5 cm) of turquoise wire. Wrap the wire 8 times around the bottom of the large loop of the link half attached to the ear wire. Trim the excess wire.

6 Repeat Steps 2 through 5 for the second earring. Oxidize the earrings in liver of sulfur (see page 30) and buff the excess oxidation with steel wool. Tumble the earrings for about 30 minutes to work-harden and polish.

MOLTEN

MATERIALS

Spool of 16-gauge pure copper square wire, about 11' (3.4 m) used

6 copper-colored 18mm polymer clay rounds

1 copper-colored 2⅛" (5.4 cm) polymer clay donut

4 gray 13mm mammoth bone rounds

4 brown 8mm African pipestone rondelles

TOOLS

Chain-nose pliers

Flat-nose pliers

Round-nose pliers

Stepped pliers or steel mandrels, 5 mm and 7 mm

Flush cutters

Flat hand file

Paper

Scissors

Chasing hammer

Rawhide mallet

Steel bench block

Sharpie

Liver of sulfur

Steel wool, #0000

Rotary tumbler with mixed stainless-steel shot

Ruler

FINISHED LENGTH

22½" (57 cm)

CHRISTINE DAMM

The strong forged look of these Sliding Rings copper links pair well with beads that reflect Earth's elemental nature. The polymer beads and focal express the colors of metal and fire, in contrast to the stony textures of the bone and pipestone beads. Pyrite, ceramic, rough-cut gemstone, or raku beads would work as well with this substantial link.

FEATURED LINK
Sliding Rings (page 46)

1 Make 6 Sliding Rings links (see page 46); set aside.

2 Make a pattern for the bail. Cut a strip of paper ¼" (6 mm) wide and 3" (7.5 cm) long; fit it around your focal donut through the hole from inside to outside. With a Sharpie, mark each side of the paper at the edge of the donut. Add at least ½" (1.3 cm) to each side for clearance and to be able to make simple end loops the size of those in the link instructions.

3 Using the measurement you just determined, flush-cut one piece of the 16-gauge copper square wire to test the size. File both ends smooth. At the mark you made on your round-nose pliers for the Sliding Rings link, form a simple loop at each end of the wire, with the opening of the loops on the same side of the wire. Mark the middle of the wire with a Sharpie. Using a barrel of the stepped pliers that is slightly larger than the thickness of your donut, grasp the mark in the middle of the jaws. Using your fingers, bend each side of the wire up vertically around the barrel of the pliers into a U-shape. Try out the shaped wire on your donut. Make sure the loops extend about ½" (1.3 cm) beyond the outer edge of the donut and are even with each other. If the length of the wire seems in good proportion to the size and thickness of the donut, make 2 more.

4 Working from the spool, make 2 jump rings (see page 25) with the 16-gauge wire using the 7 mm barrel of the stepped pliers. Open 1 jump ring and pass it through the 3 simple loops on the front of the bail; close the jump ring. Repeat, on the back of the bail.

5 Working from the spool, make 3 jump rings with the 16-gauge wire using the 5 mm barrel of the stepped piers. Open 1 jump ring and close it around the 3 vertical wires on the front of the bail; repeat with the remaining 2 jump rings. These will keep the 3 front bail wires aligned.

6 Make the clasp. Cut 2" (5 cm) of the 16-gauge wire. File both ends smooth. Form a simple loop at one end using the mark on the round-nose pliers as in the link instructions. Measure 1" (2.5 cm) from the loop and make a 90° bend with the chain-nose pliers facing away from the loop. Grasp the tail of the wire with the 7 mm barrel of the stepped pliers and bend the wire back toward the small loop to form a hook for the clasp. Turn the very end of the hook in to complete; set aside.

7 Working from the spool, make 7 jump rings using the 16-gauge wire and the 5 mm barrel of the stepped pliers. Set aside.

8 Oxidize all of the links, the bail, clasp, jump rings, and the remaining 16-gauge wire with liver of sulfur (see page 30). Buff the excess oxidation with steel wool. Add all but the extra wire to the tumbler for 1 hour to work-harden and polish.

9 Cut six 1½" (3.8 cm) lengths of the 16-gauge wire. File the ends. With round-nose pliers, form a small simple loop at one end of one wire, string 1 polymer round, and form a second simple loop at the other end of the wire. Trim the second end of the wire if necessary to make the loops the same size. Make a total of 6 polymer links.

10 Cut two 2" (5 cm) lengths of the 16-gauge wire. File the ends smooth. Form a small simple loop on one end of one wire and string 1 bone round, 2 pipestone rondelles, and 1 bone round. Form a second simple loop at the other end of the wire, trimming any excess. Repeat for a total of 2 bone/pipestone links.

11 Assemble the right side of the necklace, beginning with the focal donut. Place the wire bail around the donut and gently press the two 7mm bail jump rings toward each other, gently curving the

bail around the donut. Open one 5mm jump ring and connect both 7mm bail jump rings to one end of 1 Sliding Rings link; close. Open the large jump ring on the other end of the Sliding Rings link and attach it to a loop on 1 polymer link; close. Open one 5mm jump ring and connect the free loop on the polymer link to a loop on 1 bone/pipestone link; close. Open one 5mm jump ring and connect the free loop on the bone/pipestone link to a loop on a second polymer link; close. Open the large jump ring on the end of a second Sliding Rings link and attach it to the free loop on the second polymer link; close.

Open the large jump ring on the opposite end of the second Sliding Rings link and attach it to a loop on a third polymer link; close. Open the large jump ring on the end of a third Sliding Rings link and attach it to the free loop on the third polymer link; close. Open a 5mm jump ring and connect the other end of the third Sliding Rings link to the small simple loop on the hook clasp; close.

12 Repeat Step 11 for the left side of the necklace, using the large jump ring on the end of the last Sliding Rings link as the other half of the clasp.

MATERIALS

4½' (1.4 m) of 16-gauge pure copper wire

2 copper 9.5mm (OD/outer diameter) jump rings

10 copper 7mm (OD/outer diameter) jump rings

5 mottled pink/purple 13mm lampwork beads

5 purple 10mm lampwork beads

8 charoite 15mm coin beads

5 copper 10mm bead caps

6 transparent 8° purple seed beads

8 amethyst 10mm barrels

6 oxidized 3mm copper rounds

8 opal pink 4mm Czech glass rounds

9 copper 9mm daisy spacers

27 purple 5mm glass daisy spacers

8 lavender three-cornered 7mm Czech glass bell flowers

19 matte pink four-cornered 9mm Czech glass bell flowers

53 oxidized 21-gauge 2" (5 cm) brass head pins

Clasp of your choice

TOOLS

Chain-nose pliers

Flat-nose pliers

Round-nose pliers

Stepped pliers, 5 mm

Steel mandrels, 8 mm and 13 mm

Flush cutters

Flat file

Rawhide mallet

Steel bench block

Liver of sulfur

Steel wool, #0000

Rotary tumbler with mixed stainless-steel shot

Ruler

FINISHED LENGTH

8½" (21.5 cm)

PURPLE PASSION

LORI ANDERSON

Purple is indeed my passion when it comes to color! This classic-looking bracelet made with Engagement Ring links is the perfect backdrop for any color of bead and would look equally lovely with unoxidized metal. Load the links with charms and make yourself a real showpiece.

FEATURED LINK
Engagement Ring (page 38)

1 Make 8 Engagement Ring links (see page 38) with 16-gauge copper wire, except use a 13 mm mandrel instead of a Sharpie. Using an 8 mm mandrel, make 1 additional link to use as a charm. If desired, oxidize the links with liver of sulfur (see page 30). Buff with steel wool to remove the excess oxidization. Tumble the links to work-harden and polish.

2 Using flat-nose pliers, open the simple loops as you would a jump ring on each of the eight 13mm Engagement Ring links. Attach the simple loops on one link to the "ring" on another link; close the simple loops. Repeat, attaching all 8 Engagement Ring links in a chain. Connect two closed 7mm jump rings to the simple loops on the last link in the chain; close the simple loops. Open 2 more 7mm jump rings and attach them to the previous 7mm jump rings and the loop on the toggle ring; close the jump rings. Repeat on the opposite end of the bracelet, attaching 2 sets of 7mm jump rings and the toggle bar to the "ring" of the link.

3 Attach two 7mm jump rings to the pair of jump rings next to the toggle ring. Attach two 9.5mm jump rings to the 7mm jump rings. Open the simple loops of the 8mm Engagement Ring link and attach them to the 9.5mm jump rings; close the simple loops. This will create a charm.

4 Add dangles to the charm. On 3 head pins, string 1 purple glass daisy spacer and 1 matte pink bell flower. On a fourth head

pin, string 1 purple seed bead, 1 bead cap, 1 purple lampwork bead, and 1 copper round. On a fifth head pin, string 1 purple seed bead, 1 copper daisy spacer, 1 pink/purple lampwork bead, and 1 copper round. Attach all 5 head pins to the "ring" of the 8mm Engagement Ring link charm using wrapped loops (see page 23).

5 Make the bracelet dangles. String each of the following stacks onto a head pin:

- head pin a: 4mm opal pink round, 7mm lavender bell flower; make a total of 8.

- head pin b: amethyst barrel; make a total of 8.

- head pin c: purple seed bead, copper bead cap, purple lampwork bead, copper round; make a total of 4.

- head pin d: purple glass daisy spacer, copper daisy spacer, pink/purple lampwork bead, copper daisy spacer, purple glass daisy spacer; make a total of 4.

- head pin e: purple glass daisy spacer and matte pink bell flower; make a total of 16.

- head pin f: charoite coin bead; make a total of 8.

6 Starting on the toggle ring side of the bracelet, attach the following 6 head pins, in the order listed, to

TIP

To make a more lush version of this bracelet, make smaller Engagement Ring links and connect charms to both sides of the rings.

links 1, 3, 5, and 7 with a wrapped loop: head pins a, b, d, e, f, and e. Attach the following 6 head pins, in the order listed, to links 2, 4, 6, and 8 with a wrapped loop: head pins a, b, c, e, f, and e.

MATERIALS

10' (3 m) of 16-gauge sterling silver dead-soft wire

6' (1.8 m) of 18-gauge sterling silver dead-soft wire

16" (40.5 cm) of 20-gauge sterling silver half-hard wire

21' (6.4 m) of 22-gauge sterling silver half-hard wire

14 pastel (ivory, blue, lavender, green) 10mm etched lampwork rounds

7 pastel (ivory, blue, lavender, green) 13mm etched lampwork rounds

6 pastel (ivory, blue, lavender, green) 15mm etched lampwork rounds

54 sterling silver 6mm daisy spacers

TOOLS

Chain-nose pliers

Flat-nose pliers

Round-nose pliers

Stepped pliers or steel mandrels, 7 mm and 8 mm

Coiling tool or steel mandrel, 2 mm

Flush cutters

Chasing hammer

Rawhide mallet

Steel bench block

Sharpie (or 12 mm mandrel)

Liver of sulfur

Steel wool, #0000

Rotary tumbler with mixed stainless-steel shot

Ruler

FINISHED LENGTH

39" (99 cm)

SOJOURN BY THE SEA

CINDY WIMMER

Wear this as a statement piece or an everyday accessory. Either way, this necklace is a wirework showcase! The etched lampwork beads in the necklace are reminiscent of the pale color palette found in New England coastal cottages. Sun-bleached shells and the sound of seagulls came to mind as I created this necklace, link by beautiful link.

FEATURED LINKS

Corona (page 60)
Coiled Horseshoe (page 58)
Spiral Swirl (page 88)

1 Make 3 Corona links (see page 60), 6 Coiled Horseshoe links (see page 58), and 3 Spiral Swirl links (see page 88). Using the 8 mm barrel on the stepped pliers and 16-gauge wire, make 20 jump rings (see page 25). Using the 7 mm barrel on the stepped pliers and 16-gauge wire, make 12 jump rings.

2 For the clasp, create a 1½" (3.8 cm) long coil (see page 24) using the coiling tool and all of the 20-gauge wire. Cut 4½" (11.5 cm) of 16-gauge wire: On one end, form a small loop using the tip of the round-nose pliers. Center the loop and slide the coil onto the other end of the wire. Form a wrapped loop (see page 23) at the top of the coil and create a spiral (see page 27) with the tail of the wrapping wire, continuing until the spiral overlaps the coil. Gently press the coil around the Sharpie to create a hook.

3 Oxidize the jump rings, wire links, daisy spacers, clasp, and the remaining coil of 16-gauge wire in liver of sulfur (see page 30). Buff the excess oxidization from the jump rings, wire links, and clasp with steel wool. Tumble for 1 to 2 hours to work-harden and polish.

4 Create lampwork links with the pre-oxidized 16-gauge wire. It is preferable to work directly from the spool of wire to minimize waste. Mark the barrel of the round-nose pliers in the center with the Sharpie. Make all of the wire loops at this point to maintain a consistent size. String one 15mm lampwork round onto the 16-gauge wire. Grasp the tip of the wire at the mark on the round-nose pliers and make a simple loop (see page 22). Push the bead down to the loop. Measure and flush-cut the spool end of the wire to ⅝" (1.5 cm) from the bead. Form a second simple loop on this end. Repeat for the remaining five 15mm lampwork beads.

5 Connect the small and medium lampwork links to each other in sets of 3 by opening and closing simple loops as you would a jump ring. Open one simple loop of a 13mm lampwork link and connect it to one loop of a same-color 10mm lampwork link; close the loop. Repeat on the other end of the 13mm lampwork link. Repeat this step, creating a total of 7 sets of like-colored beads.

6 Assemble the jump rings and links. Open one 8mm jump ring and connect a second 8mm jump ring; close. Create 5 sets of linked 8mm jump rings; set aside. Create 5 additional sets of linked 8mm jump rings, inserting 1 set into the loops of each of the 6 Coiled Horseshoe links before closing.

7 Open two 7mm jump rings and connect the coiled side of 2 Coiled Horseshoe links before closing. Repeat for the remaining 4 Coiled Horseshoe links. Attach two 7mm jump rings to the large loop/coiled end of each of the 3 Corona links.

8 Assemble the necklace. Attach the simple loop on the end of one 3-bead component (10mm–13mm–10mm) to the hook clasp. Attach the simple loop on the other end of the 3-bead component to a set of linked 8mm jump rings (set aside in Step 6). Repeat this sequence, attaching 4 additional 3-bead components with sets of linked 8mm jump rings between each unit. Attach the end of the last 3-bead component to the set of linked jump rings already attached to one end of a Coiled

TIPS

Ordinarily, wire jewelry made with annealed lampwork beads can go directly into the tumbler. However, I used etched lampwork beads for this project, so I decided to use caution and did not add them to the tumbler. The rotary action might have marked up the matte finish of the beads. If you are in doubt about whether a bead can be tumbled, just add one bead to the tumbler—if you can spare it—to see if the finish is adversely affected.

The extended time it takes to fashion this completely handmade necklace is well worth it as it can be worn a couple of different ways. Wear it long or double it up as a two-strand necklace.

Horseshoe link unit. Attach the set of linked jump rings on the other end of the Coiled Horseshoe link unit to another 3-bead component. Attach the other end of the 3-bead component to the simple loop of a Corona link. Attach the double jump rings of the Corona link to a 15mm bead link. Attach the other end of the 15mm bead link to a Spiral Swirl link. Attach the other end of the Spiral Swirl link to a 15mm bead link. Attach the other end of the 15mm bead link to the set of linked jump rings on a Coiled Horseshoe link unit. Attach the set of linked jump rings on the other end of the Coiled Horseshoe link unit to a 15mm bead link. Attach the other end of the 15mm bead link to the double jump rings on a Corona link. Attach the simple loop on the Corona link to a 15mm bead link. Attach the other end of

the 15mm bead link to a Spiral Swirl link. Attach the other end of the Spiral Swirl link to a 15mm bead link. Attach the other end of the 15mm bead link to the set of linked jump rings on a Coiled Horseshoe link unit. Attach the set of linked jump rings on the other end of the Coiled Horseshoe link to a 15mm bead link. Attach the other end of the 15mm bead link to the double links on a Corona link. Attach the simple loop on the Corona link to one end of the remaining 3-bead component. Attach the other end of the 3-bead component to the remaining Spiral Swirl link. Grasp the loop on the free end of the Spiral Swirl link and turn it perpendicular to the link with flat-nose pliers. Flatten the loop slightly with the chasing hammer on the bench block. This will serve as the catch for the hook clasp.

SUN & CLOUDS EARRINGS

MATERIALS

1 polymer clay 1" (2.5 cm) donut
(or gemstone, ceramic, resin, etc.)

3½' (1.1 m) of 18-gauge pure copper
wire

2 copper 18-gauge 5mm jump rings

TOOLS

Chain-nose pliers

Flat-nose pliers

Round-nose pliers

Bail-forming pliers or steel mandrel,
9 mm

Flush cutters

Sharpie

Rawhide mallet

Steel bench block

Cup burr or wire rounding tool

Liver of sulfur

Steel wool, #0000

Rotary tumbler with mixed stainless-
steel shot

Ruler

FINISHED LENGTH

3" (7.5 cm) from top of ear wire

CHRISTINE DAMM

These earrings remind me of hours spent lying on a grassy hill watching cloud shapes move across the sun. The Cumulus Clouds link combines with a polymer donut and a trio of jump rings that mimic wrapped wire. It's easy to adapt the design to the dimensions of the donut and your choice of material—gemstone, ceramic, metal, resin, or polymer.

FEATURED LINK
Cumulus Clouds (page 74)

1 Using the copper wire, make 2 Cumulus Cloud links through Step 6 of the directions on page 75. For the next step, trim the remaining vertical wire to 1¼" (3.2 cm), then grasp the wire close to the end with the round-nose pliers and form a small loop. Switch to chain-nose pliers and hold the loop while forming a spiral (see page 27) with the remaining wire. With chain-nose pliers, center the spiral under the link. Repeat on the second link.

2 Use the 9 mm mandrel to make 6 jump rings (see page 25) with the copper wire.

3 Oxidize all jump rings, links, and the remaining 18-gauge wire with liver of sulfur (see page 30) and buff the excess oxidation with steel wool. Tumble jump rings and links for 1 hour.

4 Open one 9mm jump ring, insert it through 1 donut, and close the jump ring. Repeat with two more 9mm jump rings. Open one 5mm jump ring and string it through all three 9mm jump rings and the top loop of 1 Cumulus Cloud link; close the jump ring. Repeat this step with the second donut.

5 Make the ear wires. Flush-cut 4" (10 cm) of the copper wire. Grasp one end with round-nose pliers and make a small loop. Grasp the loop with chain-nose pliers and form a small spiral (see page 27). With the spiral facing you, grasp the wire ¼" (6 mm) below the spiral with round-nose pliers. Create a hook shape by rolling your wrist forward,

until the spiral almost touches the straight wire. Fit the donut into the hook shape, with the spiral facing toward the front and the straight part of the wire pointing up at the back of the donut. Pinch the wires closed just above the donut with your fingers or chain-nose pliers to secure the donut.

6 Place the Sharpie on the edge of the donut, behind the wire on the back of the donut. Bend the wire around the Sharpie to form a hook-shaped ear wire. Flush-cut the end of the ear wire to the desired length and smooth with the cup burr or wire rounding tool. Grasp the tip of the ear wire with chain-nose pliers and bend it up slightly. Repeat Steps 5 and 6 for the second earring. Work-harden the ear wires using a rawhide mallet on the bench block.

TIP

Be sure to adjust the size of your jump rings and ear wires to accommodate the thickness of your donut.

TAMARINE

CINDY WIMMER

After completing a necklace made entirely of copper Corona links, I searched for the perfect focal piece. There it was: an impressively sized hill tribe pendant that I have held onto for years. The pendant was silver, while the links were all copper. I preferred a more harmonious blend of the two metals, so I reworked all of the links to combine both metals. One of the pleasures of working with wire is that you can customize the gauge and color—in this case, to complement a focal that was tucked away, awaiting just the right design!

FEATURED LINK
Corona (page 60)

MATERIALS
30' (9.1 m) of 22-gauge pure copper wire

10' (3 m) of 18-gauge sterling silver dead-soft wire

3½" (9 cm) of 16-gauge pure copper wire

55mm hill tribe silver pendant

Sterling silver clasp hook of your choice

TOOLS
Chain-nose pliers

Flat-nose pliers

Long round-nose pliers

Round-nose pliers

Coiling tool or steel mandrel, 2 mm

Flush cutters

Flat hand file

Rawhide mallet

Steel bench block

Sharpie (or 12 mm mandrel)

Liver of sulfur

Steel wool, #0000

Rotary tumbler with mixed stainless-steel shot

Ruler

FINISHED LENGTH
18" (45.5 cm)

1 Make 18 Corona links (see page 60). Oxidize the links in liver of sulfur (see page 30) and buff the excess oxidation with steel wool. Tumble the links for about 1 hour.

2 Make a bail for the pendant. Place the middle of the 16-gauge wire in the back of the round-nose pliers. Wrap the wires in opposite directions, forming a loop around the back barrel of the pliers, until the tail wires are in a straight line. Remove the loop from the pliers and open it slightly. String the pendant onto the loop and pinch the loop closed with chain-nose pliers. Hold the loop facing you and grasp one tail wire close to the loop with chain-nose pliers; bend the wire forward 90°. Repeat on the other tail wire so both wires are facing forward. Trim the wires to ⅞" (2.2 cm) and file the ends smooth. Grasp the tail wires with the back of the long round-nose pliers and roll forward to create simple loops (see page 22) on either side.

3 Open one of the simple loops on the bail and attach it to the coiled loop section of a Corona link. Open the simple loop on the Corona link and attach it to the coiled section of another Corona link. Continue to create a chain by adding 7 more Corona links. Repeat on the other side of the necklace. There should be 9 Corona links per side.

4 Open the simple loop on the last Corona link on one side of the necklace and attach it to a wire clasp of your choice. Use the simple loop on the last Corona link on the opposite side of the necklace as an eye for the clasp.

JEWELRY PROJECT RESOURCES

AFTERNOON IN ANNAPOLIS

Bare round and twisted red brass wire: Fundametals, fundametals.net; *blue topaz beads:* Rings & Things, rings-things.com; *brass 2mm beads:* Hands of the Hills, hohbead.com; *brass 7mm bead caps:* Vintage Jewelry Supply, vintagejewelrysupplies.com; *crimp tubes and crimp covers:* check your local bead store; *all other gemstones:* ibexpos, innovativebeadsexpos.com.

AMBER SKIES

Brass collar blank: Objects and Elements, objectsandelements.com; *faceted gemstones:* j. Nic Loft, jnicloft .etsy.com.

BUZZ ME IN

Lampwork button and hollow glass bead: Kerry Bogert, kabsconcepts.com; *flexible beading wire, crimp beads, and seed beads:* available at your local bead store.

CREATE YOUR DREAM

Waxed Irish linen: Royalwood, royalwoodltd.com; *dotted circle component and S-clasp:* Dry Gulch Beads and Jewelry, drygulch.com; *All gemstone beads:* Fire Mountain Gems & Beads, firemountaingems.com; *Oval copper stamping charm and 3mm silver crimp tubes:* Beadaholique, beadaholique .com; *Silver-filled wire:* Monsterslayer, monsterslayer.com.

DOWN TO EARTH

Crimp-end clasp: Artbeads, artbeads .com; *leather cord:* Leather Cord USA, leathercordusa.com; *copper nugget beads:* ZNETSHOWS Inc., Znetshows .com; *potato pearls and silver nugget beads:* Fire Mountain Gems & Beads, firemountaingems.com.

ODE TO DOWNTON ABBEY

Similar antique buckle: Etsy, antiques malls, flea markets; *coin pearl teardrops:* International Gem and Jewelry Show Inc., intergem .com; *mother-of-pearl beads:* Rings & Things, rings-things.com; *brass bead caps:* Vintage Jewelry Supplies, vintagejewelrysupplies.com; *mother-of-pearl rose beads:* Gemme Tresor, gemmetresor.etsy.com; *findings:* available at your local bead store.

GINGKO

Ceramic gingko pendant: Shaterra, shaterra.etsy.com; *copper jump rings:* Artbeads, artbeads.com; *Kazuri beads:* Antelope Beads, antelopebeads.com; *vintage acrylic beads:* Black Sheep Beads, blacksheepbeads.etsy.com; *sari silk ribbon:* Etsy, etsy.com.

GRAND BAZAAR

Pancake spacer beads: Hip Chick Beads, hipchickbeads.com; *turquoise bead:* China Mountain Gem Inc., cmtbeads .com; *Tibetan, hill tribe, kyanite tube and all other silver beads:* International Gem and Jewelry Show Inc., intergem .com; *crimp covers:* Monsterslayer, monsterslayer.com; *Twisted Tornado crimps:* Via Murano, viamurano.com.

GREEN WITH INFINITY

Crystal rondelles: Goody Beads, goodybeads.com; *oval jump rings:* Rio Grande Jewelry Supply Co., riogrande .com; *rhinestone connector and dangle:* The Vintage Jewel, thevintagejewel .etsy.com; *similar vintage brooch and rhinestone bracelet:* Etsy, antiques malls, flea markets.

MAGICIAN'S RINGS

Lampwork glass beads: Kerry Bogert, kabsconepts.com; *anodized copper wire:* Paramount Wire Co., parawire .com.

GENERAL WIREWORKING RESOURCES

MOLTEN

Mammoth bone bead and African pipestone disc beads: Happy Mango Beads, happymangobeads.com; *polymer clay donut focal and beads:* Christine Damm, storiestheytell.etsy.com; *square copper wire:* Monsterslayer, monsterslayer.com.

PURPLE PASSION

Amethyst barrels, charoite: check your local bead store; *copper rounds and jump rings, Czech glass bell flowers, daisy spacers, bead caps, and head pins:* Artbeads, artbeads.com; *lampwork beads:* Lori Anderson, beadsoupkits.com.

SOJOURN BY THE SEA

Daisy spacers: Artbeads, artbeads.com; *lampwork beads:* Amber Van Meter, naosglass.com.

SUN & CLOUDS EARRINGS

Polymer clay donuts: Christine Damm, storiestheytell.etsy.com.

TAMARINE

Hill tribe pendant: International Gem and Jewelry Show Inc., intergem.com.

BEADUCATION INC.

beaducation.com
Wire, oxidizing solutions, tools, tumblers

ETSY

etsy.com
Wire, vintage components

FUNDAMETALS.NET

fundametals.net
Wire, oxidizing solutions, tools

METALLIFEROUS

metalliferous.com
Wire, oxidizing solutions, tools

MONSTERSLAYER

monsterslayer.com
Wire, tools, stringing materials

PARAMOUNT WIRE CO.

parawire.com
Colored wire

RIO GRANDE

riogrande.com
Wire, tools, oxidizing solutions

THUNDERBIRD SUPPLY

Thunderbirdsupply.com
Wire, tools, tumblers, stringing materials

CONTRIBUTORS

Author

CINDY WIMMER

cindywimmer.com

Cindy Wimmer is a jewelry designer with a passion for mingling vintage elements with modern wire design. Her jewelry has been published in both national and international trade publications. She has contributed designs to the books *Wire Style 2* (Interweave, 2011) and *Bead Soup* (Kalmbach, 2012). Cindy is the cofounder of artBLISS, which hosts jewelry and mixed-media workshops in the D.C. area. Antiquing, baking, and family adventures are among her favorite things in the world. She lives in Virginia with her husband and four sons. *The Missing Link* is her first book.

Contributors

LORI ANDERSON

prettythingsblog.com

Lori Anderson is a jewelry designer and blogger who is best known for her annual Bead Soup Blog Party. She enjoys featuring handmade beads in her work, and her designs have been published in numerous magazines. Lori is the author of *Bead Soup* (Kalmbach, 2012). She lives with her husband and son on the eastern shore of Maryland.

KERRY BOGERT

kabsconcepts.com

Kerry Bogert is a mom, author, artist, and designer living in western New York with her high-school–sweetheart husband and their three kids. When she isn't making her own glass beads, she is coming up with new ways to show off lampwork in colorful, creative jewelry. Look for her books, *Totally Twisted* (Interweave, 2010) and *Rustic Wrappings* (Interweave, 2012).

DIANE COOK

rosajosies.com

Diane Cook is a jewelry designer and mixed-media artist. Her love for using vintage jewelry in her designs, especially vintage rhinestones, has become an ever-constant source of inspiration. Diane has been published in *Belle Armoire Jewelry*, *Artful Blogging*, *Somerset Memories*, *Jewelry Affaire*, *Marie*, and *Jewelry the zine*. She was honored to be a guest curator for Crescendoh.com and teaches at major art retreats locally as well as nationally. Diane lives with her husband in Texas.

CHRISTINE DAMM

storiestheytell.com

Christine Damm can't recall a time in her life when she was not drawing or sewing or doing something with her hands. She has been a potter, a dressmaker, a textile designer, and a graphic artist. Christine is a storyteller who believes as our lives tell a story, so does our art. Christine studied art at New York University and the School for American Craftsmen at the Rochester Institute of Technology. Her polymer clay jewelry was featured in a *Belle Armoire Jewelry Designer Showcase* in 2011 and appears regularly in jewelry magazines, books, and blogs. She teaches at the artBLISS retreat in Virginia and at her home studio in Vermont.

TRACY STATLER

tracystatler.com

Tracy Statler is a self-taught jewelry designer who began making jewelry nine years ago. She enjoys making stylish and comfortable pieces that incorporate natural elements such as gemstones, wood beads, and soft stringing materials such as leather and Irish linen. Bracelets are her favorite type of jewelry to make. Her jewelry has been published in *Bohemian-Inspired Jewelry* (Interweave, 2012). She writes about making jewelry on her blog and lives in northern Virginia with her husband and two children.

INDEX

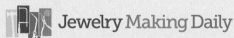